IMAGES OF THE BRITISH RAILWAY LANDSCAPE

ICONIC SCENES OF TRAINS AND ARCHITECTURE

DAVID GOODYEAR

PEN & SWORD TRANSPORT

AN IMPRINT OF PEN & SWORD BOOKS LTD.
YORKSHIRE - PHILADELPHIA

Front Cover:
Top picture: Corfe Common, Swanage Railway. Class 26 26007 passes with an early afternoon train from Norden to Swanage, 9 May 2009.
Bottom picture: Brunel's Royal Albert Bridge is crossed by Great Western's "Castle" HST with power car 43094 *St Mawes Castle* leading the 19.36 Plymouth to Penzance,12 July 2020.

Rear cover:
Main picture: Corfe Common, Swanage Railway. LSWR Drummond design Class M7 0-4-4T 30053 climbs away with the 13.30 Norden to Harman's Cross, 7 July 2007

First published in Great Britain in 2022 by
Pen and Sword Transport
An imprint of
Pen & Sword Books Ltd
Yorkshire - Philadelphia

Copyright © David Goodyear, 2022

ISBN 978 1 39901 130 3

Typeset in 11/14 Palatino by SJmagic DESIGN SERVICES, India.

Printed and bound in India by Replika Press Pvt. Ltd.

Pen & Sword Books Ltd incorporates the Imprints of Pen & Sword Books Archaeology, Atlas, Aviation, Battleground, Discovery, Family History, History, Maritime, Military, Naval, Politics, Railways, Select, Transport, True Crime, Fiction, Frontline Books, Leo Cooper, Praetorian Press, Seaforth Publishing, Wharncliffe and White Owl.

For a complete list of Pen & Sword titles please contact

PEN & SWORD BOOKS LIMITED
47 Church Street, Barnsley, South Yorkshire, S70 2AS, England
E-mail: enquiries@pen-and-sword.co.uk
Website: www.pen-and-sword.co.uk

or

PEN AND SWORD BOOKS
1950 Lawrence Rd, Havertown, PA 19083, USA
E-mail: Uspen-and-sword@casematepublishers.com
Website: www.penandswordbooks.com

CONTENTS

FOREWORD

The railway landscape that we have inherited in the UK is strongly influenced by the waterways and rivers that preceded the building of the railways. Canals especially provided an easy way for moving goods such as coal and wool directly to the mills where they would be used in the manufacturing process and the completed products then shipped onwards for the business of trade and supply. A splendid example of this is Saddleworth Viaduct which crosses the Huddersfield Narrow Canal, as seen here near Lime Kiln Lock. It has twenty-three semi-circular arches and follows a gentle curve as it supports trains climbing towards or descending from the Pennines. The Huddersfield Narrow Canal was one of the canals opened in the late eighteenth

Saddleworth Viaduct and Huddersfield Narrow Canal feature Lime Kiln Lock and Saddleworth Upper Mill Viaduct.

century expansion in the waterways system to meet the change that was sweeping the industries of Lancashire and Yorkshire.

Each railway landscape incorporates a story of its past, be it of a viaduct crossing a historic quay, a quaint country station with the waiting rooms and ticket offices often now providing a comfortable home, a steam locomotive proudly displaying the company livery, or a narrow gauge line following the contours of hills and mountains moulded by the creative forces of nature that raised them up. Saddleworth represents such a typical example where the history of the viaduct is revealed in its aesthetic design and also contributes an integral aspect of the landscape into which it fits. The grandeur of a steam train traversing the Settle and Carlisle railway within the context of the raw nature of the Yorkshire Dales all but emphasises the bleak and rugged scenery for which it is so famous. The depth of admiration for such scenes has occasionally been referred to as the 'romance of the railways' – a term often applied to steam locomotives which make their presence known through their white, or black, exhaust that escapes as the living being hisses and snorts while hauling its heavy load. Equally, a smart newly-painted electric unit escaping the dark pitch of Birmingham New Street station conveys a sense of its cityscape surroundings as it sets out on a journey through lightless tunnels and onwards through a post-industrial Black Country. Sleek new trains add their own quality to their location, yet even a mundane diesel unit can enhance its location as an integral expression of the local train as it rolls along a riverside or through a suburban setting.

Modern and historic railways in this way combine to offer a picturesque tapestry of how our landscape interweaves with the trains which travel through it. The mystery contained within these vastly contrasting landscapes, be they nature's scenic display or an industrial man-made complex, is unfurled as these trains pass through with their intrepid explorers eagerly journeying onwards, seeking all that may be revealed. The photographs in this book provide a brief glimpse into the rich cultural and awesome treasure awaiting our adventure. I hope to share this journey with you and maybe you too will find a sense of awe and wonder in exploring this portrayal of modern and preserved railways. "Please note that the featured preserved locomotives where referred to in captions are shown in ownership of the named railway at the time of the photograph".

My thanks to my wife Valerie for offering an additional 'eye' in my choice of photographs and to Gareth Harrison for offering his professional slant and discrete honesty when requested.

Chapter 1

THE MODERN RAILWAY LANDSCAPE

College Wood Viaduct: Great Western Class 150/2 150246 crosses with a late afternoon service from Falmouth Docks to Truro, 21 July 2020.

Passengers are afforded a grandstand view over Penryn River towards Flushing from this fine viaduct. Cornwall is in the *Guinness Book of Rail Facts and Feats* for having the greatest number of railway viaducts per mile on a British railway – in the seventy-five miles of main line between Saltash and Penzance there are thirty-four viaducts, although this viaduct is not one of those, being along the branch line. This unusually high number of viaducts is unsurprising in view of the many rivers, creeks and inlets which enhance the scenic beauty of Cornwall's landscape, which inevitably attracts the attention of summertime visitors who descend on favoured ports and towns such as Falmouth.

Golant: British Rail (BR) Class 4MT 2-6-0 76079 hauls the 16.45 Plymouth to Fowey, 'The Fowey Pony', operated by Past Times Railtours, 29 May 2006.

   The residents of the local village here are more used to seeing and hearing china clay freight trains and no doubt raise more than an eyebrow at the crowds of besieging photographers who converge at this location when such rare events occur as this, when a steam train wends its way down the branch and trundles past the moored boats while crossing the causeway. Indeed there will be an array of cameras pointed at this rare event from the field to the back of this photographer. The weather has decided to cooperate and yet it's not too warm for a wisp of steam to make its presence known. Once the train has returned from its nearby destination of Fowey, there will be a mass exit of contented rail enthusiasts, having gazed on this serene scene and warmly welcomed its guest visitor.

Golant: EWS Class 66 66248 returns Pathfinder Tours' 'Western China Clay' excursion from Carne Point, Fowey, towards Lostwithiel, 19 March 2005.

Creeks and coastal estuaries with gently rolling hills dipping down to the calm marine blue waters of inlets sheltered from the nearby swell of the Atlantic sea all combine to attract many visitors to Cornwall. The reward is clearly seen here for this train of fortunate visiting travellers from the London area, basking in the early sunshine of spring, as it potters along the causeway of this normally freight-only line which usually conveys loaded china clay trains to the awaiting ships at Fowey Harbour. The small boats await the lure of a higher tide and the warmer days that summer will surely bring.

Sandplace: First Great Western Class 153 153318 in 'Heart of Wessex Line' promotional livery is seen operating the 13.45 Liskeard to Looe service, 9 February 2008.

The bare nature of this winter landscape is vividly portrayed, with trees stripped of their leafy canopy and all seems to be in hibernation. Yet a sense of quiet and peace is expressed here as the single railcar, more than adequate for the passenger demand at this time of year, meanders around one of the many curves of a branch line characterised by the streams and woodlands that it follows, past Cornish white-bleached cottages – and all lit by the subdued light provided by a cold winter's sun. It is as if everything, including the passengers on board, seeks the stronger light of spring that is hinted at just around the corner.

Opposite: Sandplace: First Great Western Class 153 153318 in 'Heart of Wessex Line' promotional livery passes from woodland to the upper reaches of the estuary with a mid-afternoon service from Liskeard to Looe, 9 February 2008.

Captured through the woodland branches that define this 'branch line', the single diesel unit arrives on a scene which promises the river's descent to the coastal harbour at Looe. A welcome blue sky is reflected in the marshland waters at a time of year when any sunlight is short-lived and the shadows from the surrounding Cornish hills are already encroaching. The train is a guest of the scene into which it arrives and seems a welcome adjunct to the red and yellow hues that surround it.

Below: Terras Crossing: First Great Western Class 153 153325 in 'Citizensrail' advertising livery is seen here approaching Terras Crossing on the Looe Branch with a mid-afternoon train, 8 May 2017.

The Looe Valley is at its best in spring and autumn when the vivid and varied tapestry of green colours expressed in the trees and hillsides of the lush valley reflect in the tidal waters of the river as it curves its way gently through the rolling Cornish countryside. The branch line service is adequate for a single railcar in winter, although it requires a two-car unit in the height of summer, for the number of passengers is always much greater when the sun shines at the coastal and seaside harbour of Looe at the mouth of this river. The advertising livery provides a bright and exuberant contrast to its surroundings.

Above: Terras crossing: First Great Western Class 150/2 150239 operating the 15.15 Liskeard to Looe service, 19 July 2008.

The image portrayed on the signpost might be wishful thinking although there have been, all be it very rarely, steam locomotives and steam railcars along this branch within the last decade. Of course there is much yearning for a repeat visit. However, the more ordinary Class 150 and 153 units fulfil the mainstay of the services to the popular resort of Looe. Their reversal at Coombe Junction always provides interest for observant passengers, because this train must change direction in order to ascend to Liskeard on the 1 in 60 gradient opened in May 1901. As often the case, Looe may be basking in sunshine on the coast but the clouds are gathering over Caradon and threaten to bring a shower of rain timed perfectly for when the passengers must leave the train at Liskeard.

Opposite below: Terras crossing: First Great Western Class 153 153318 in 'Heart of Wessex Line' promotional livery arrives at Terras crossing with the 15.49 Looe to Liskeard, 9 February 2008.

At high tide, the causeway to the left of the railway level crossing is regularly covered by seawater, and the railway is sometimes closed when spring tides are particularly high. The railcar must halt and sound a warning hoot before it proceeds, a necessity as the turning from the main road is immediately to the right of the crossing. Yet this train strides along the low embankment oblivious to the incoming tide. Passengers on board can afford a reflective moment to take in the beauty of the scene as they pause alongside the tranquil tidal waters. The train creates its own reflection as it recommences the journey further along the valley. Such a vista is a rare treat indeed –an expression of the romance of the railway, for who can fail to fall for its lure.

Below: Near Sandplace: First Great Western Class 150/2 150239 operates the 19.11 Liskeard to Looe, 19 July 2008.

This summer evening train passes alongside the East Looe River estuary near its upper limit. The gently rolling Cornish hills are bathed in the last rays of sunshine and the seaside crowds will by now have made their journeys home or to their holiday accommodation. Passengers on board may well find that there is still the opportunity to find a traditional fish and chip supper and a fine pint of Cornish brewed IPA in Looe while the branch line succumbs to the onset of the approaching shadows and the tranquil calm of the countryside after a busy day conveying the contented travellers.

Opposite: Near St Germans: A 'Castle' Class HST set climbs towards Menheniot with a springtime early afternoon train for Penzance, 7 May 2020.

The Cornish landscape in spring is unrivalled with its display of hedgerows bustling with colours and hues of wild flowers and, of course, the famed bluebell. The rolling hills beckon to the western edges of Dartmoor and higher ground, hiding where the cloud bubbles up as the day's warmth builds. The distinctive green livery of the train fits in with the springtime green to express the verdant energy in the revitalised nature that surrounds it. Its intervention into the pastoral setting is thus entirely justified.

Below: St Germans Viaduct: Colas Class 70 70802 crosses the viaduct with the Moorswater to Aberthaw return cement train, 19 January 2017.

The COLAS-operated cement workings into Cornwall guaranteed Class 70 locomotives, and added an attractive splash of colour at any time of year; the gentle winter's lighting especially helps to draw out the natural wonder of this tidal harbour and viaduct. The graceful seventeen arches that uphold this long viaduct stand resolute and pensive, expressing the promise of carrying safely to intended dream-holiday destinations those many holidaymakers who in times past have travelled down on the 'Cornish Riviera' or such other grand trains that allowed them to escape the dirt and grime of their industrial workplaces. The glimpsed scene would surely whet their appetite for the tranquillity and calm offered amidst Cornwall's picture-postcard scenery.

Opposite: Calstock Viaduct: A First Great Western Class 153 crosses over the magnificent viaduct with its twelve 60ft wide arches, 850ft long, 20 December 2009.

This brooding yet gentle viaduct links Devon and Cornwall, with a proudly determined stride across the River Tamar which at this point is still tidal. Here the steep sides of the Tamar valley emphasise the 120ft height of the viaduct, from which the train has to climb steeply away at either side. It is as if the viaduct cradles the single railcar in its journey across, a safe haven amidst dramatic scenery.

Below: Saltash: The Royal Albert Bridge is crossed by 'The Great Britain' 12.54 Penzance to Bristol operated by the Railway Touring Company. The front locomotive is GWR 'King' 6000 Class 4-6-0 6024 *King Edward I*; second is GWR 'Castle' 4073 Class 4-6-0 5051 *Earl Bathurst*, 7 April 2007.

Isambard Kingdom Brunel's engineering triumph, seen in the impressive yet graceful sweep of the western main span's wrought iron tubular arch, greets the triumph of Great Western steam in the 'King' Class locomotive. While this class of steam locomotive was banned over the bridge, there are reliable reports from local railway historians conveying eye-witness accounts and experiences suggesting that they did indeed cross the bridge on rare exceptions, such as in trials, and in traffic movements associated with the Blitz on Plymouth. The two locomotives portray admirably the splendour of steam, and their awesome tribute to Brunel is to be applauded.

Saltash: the Royal Albert Bridge, Hanson Traction Class 56s: the front locomotive is 56312 *Artemis* and the second is 56311, which here combine to double-head Pathfinder Tours' return 'The Cornishman' 16.13 Penzance to Tame Bridge across the Royal Albert Bridge, 26 June 2010.

Brunel's Royal Albert Bridge, opened 2 May 1859, is an architectural masterpiece and at the same time an astonishing feat of engineering. Built where the River Tamar narrows, seventy feet deep at high water here, it needed to allow sufficient height for sailing ships to pass underneath. This two-span bowstring suspension bridge, with each of its two main spans as a wrought iron tubular arch, ever-fascinates both viewers and traversing travellers, and is evocative of an age when such engineering features expressed the epitome of achievement and creative genius. While breathtaking in itself, it offers eye-catching vistas upstream towards western Dartmoor and downstream towards Devonport, and also westwards to the natural beauty of the River Lynher estuary. Both of these Class 56s returned to the main line in late 2008 and have seen use with Colas Rail, working on the Washwood Heath to Immingham and Boston to Washwood Heath steel workings, Dagenham to Dollands Moor 'Transfesa' trains and Dollands Moor to Hams Hall Norfolk Line container workings.

Saltash: the Royal Albert Bridge. First Great Western HST with power car 43140 leading, and 43016 at rear, passes with the 17.18 Newquay to London Paddington service, 26 June 2010.

A vista of the cool blue waters of the Atlantic as they flow into the Tamar estuary awaits those lucky passengers who gaze from the comfort of their High Speed Train (HST) as it crosses the border between Devon and Cornwall. On westward-bound trains, there is indeed a definite sense of moving into a county imbued with Celtic tradition and picturesque coastal harbours and beaches, and of course the famed Cornish pasty. It is as if their train is arriving as a guest of this Royal Duchy, with the promise of embracing the natural beauty of the Cornish Riviera for the duration of its stay. For the holidaymakers earnestly looking forward to arriving at their idyllic destination, their fortnight's stay will fly by and they will soon have to return east, as also with this featured train as it bids farewell to the county until its return.

Royal Albert Bridge: First Great Western Class 158 158766 at the rear of a First Great Western Class 150 operating the 15.50 Plymouth to Penzance is seen entering the bridge and passing the Royal Albert Bridge signal box (disused), 21 October 2007.

This Class 158 unit carries TransPennine Express livery, having been previously based at Neville Hill depot in Leeds, and very recently transferred to Bristol St Philips Marsh as of 2 September 2007. The Tamar Road Bridge prominent in the background was opened in 1961, replacing a ferry across to Saltash – there remains a car ferry across to Torpoint from Devonport for accessing Cornwall via Antony. Like Brunel's Royal Albert Bridge it provides an essential link for transport from Devon to Cornwall. The bridge was built using suspended construction, and the Cleveland Bridge and Engineering Company later used the same technique to construct the first Severn Bridge. It was the first major suspension bridge to be built after the war, and for a time the longest suspension bridge in England. You will need to pay a toll to cross on return to Devon but, contrary to some local rumours, you will not require your passport.

Bere Alston: First Great Western Class 153 153318 awaits departure with the 11.40 Plymouth to Gunnislake during late December's cold weather, 20 December 2009.

Traces of the London and South Western Railway (LSWR) route from Plymouth to Tavistock and Exeter via Okehampton are seen, especially on the disused down platform, despite its lack of rails, and those sleepers could be imagined as being ready for laying down for a revitalised railway service to Tavistock. Alas, while there have been various suggestions and indications about how this might be financed, and the route is protected from further intrusive building, there is no impetus to carry such a project forward and thus the only trains to be seen remain those such as this diesel unit bound for the Cornish side of the River Tamar.

Tamerton Viaduct: Hunslet-Barclay Class 20/9 20904 *Jarvis* and 20901 *Nancy* cross with the Chipman's weedkilling train, 8 April 1990.

This train had already been spraying weeds outward-bound on the Gunnislake branch and is seen on its return 'spray' journey to keep those hardy weeds from bursting into springtime flourish amidst the ballast and rails. Such trains usually run at night and hence are difficult to photograph away from brightly-lit stations. However, here they make a welcome change from the staple date of diesel multiple units and the unusual sight of Class 20s operating down a rural Devon branch. The front cab at the end of the first of the carriages used suggests a previous life as a Southern or Eastern Region electric unit driving trailer more used to conveying commuters into the city than weed-killing fluid! The inlet allows boats into the creek from the Tamar Estuary, which is quite broad at this point.

Devonport: Colas Class 70 70812 passes Her Majesty's Naval Base, Devonport, as it crosses Ford Viaduct with engineering empties on a winter morning, 19 January 2020.

Devonport Dockyard is constantly busy, playing host to shipping conveying members of the British Armed Forces while servicing and even maintaining the steady arrival of frigates, aircraft carriers and other naval vessels which call in, some of them arriving as guests from other European countries. There is even an internal dockyard railway, which has been the focus of expert comment and research by local historian Paul Burkhalter. It is as if the very duty of the train in its role of conveying engineers' wagons from weekend track maintenance complements the shared function of engineering skills which keep the railway safe, as also the skills of those working in the dockyard to support the navy in its essential protective role.

Devonport: LMS Class 5MT 4-6-0 45407 hauls Past Time Rail's 'The Harbour Master' 13.42 Plymouth to St Blazey section of the tour, 26 March 2007.

I met Plymouth's harbour master on an occasion when he kindly took part as a consultant in a team challenge for sixth-form students which I was supervising. His need to have an overview of all shipping entering and leaving the shipping lanes indicated a great sense of power and authority on his behalf, although he was very modest in his role during this event. The power and energy of this locomotive is captured through the bridge arch as it climbs the short gradient of 1 in 59 towards Devonport station and tunnel. The accompanying sound of course conveys the impression equally as much as the image but we must leave that to be imagined.

Devonport: an infrequent pairing of Class 158 158762 and 158747 forming the 12.10 Penzance to Plymouth, passing near Devonport station, 30 March 2020.

This photograph expresses the railway landscape of the town and city suburb, with its cuttings, overbridges, walled gardens, grand houses and a local diesel unit operating a stopping or semi-fast service. The line appears well maintained and expresses a railway that is both cared for and nurtured for its purpose. Use of paired Class 158 units in Cornwall had been very unusual until this date when a regular diagram was introduced which henceforth saw them working between Devon and Cornwall on a daily basis.

Hemerdon Summit: Great Western Class 800 units are seen at the top of Hemerdon with a midday service for London Paddington, 31 May 2019.

The new IETs find the climb up Hemerdon Bank to be of no challenge, with their uprated diesel engines providing a steady surge of necessary power. They simply glide up a gradient which at 1 in 42 at its steepest required passenger and freight trains to summon the assistance of banking locomotives in the days of steam. Once past Newbury, this train will take advantage of the newly electrified route to switch over to electric motors to run ever-more smoothly and swiftly to its destination. It exudes a sense of pride in fulfilling its purpose, almost boasting the very best of new technological design and manufactured features which enfold its journey along Brunel's famous West of England main line legacy.

A Cross Country HST passes through the Devon springtime countryside having just crossed Slade Viaduct, 4 April 2020.

The livery of this train matches the golden and russet colours of the spring trees and bracken, accompanied by the warm glow of the early spring sunshine. The emerging buds hint at the spring greens which will follow shortly afterwards and the green grass awaits that rich, lush colour that it will possess after receiving its share of Devon's April showers. Dartmoor in the background echoes this tribute, having weathered the winter's storms and snow. Given the choice of travelling by Cross Country on one of these infrequently diagrammed yet vastly comfortable trains or on one of the many 'Voyager' units, which are in comparison cramped and bestowed with far less seating-cushion, there is absolutely no contention.

Blachford Viaduct: A South West Trains Class 159 crosses with the 09.20 London Waterloo to Plymouth, 29 October 2009. This service was withdrawn west of Exeter after 12 December 2009.

The autumnal hues are in full flourish in this tapestry of foliage which a dense woodland displays to the passing visitor – the main stamping ground for these trains is the previous LSWR route from Exeter to London Waterloo, and this was quite an extension to their usual territory. To be truly authentic, a 'southern' service would take the route to Plymouth via Okehampton as in steam days; alas that line did not survive Beeching's scythe.

Blachford Viaduct: A First Great Western HST crosses with the 07.40 Plymouth to London Paddington service, 10 June 2006.

The bright and distinctive livery exhibited on the HST train set forming this early morning service is seen to good effect on the viaduct's north side, and contrasts with a valley where the trees are nearly engulfing the railway, clearly imposing their own takeover. Here the steep undulations mean that the land in close proximity to the viaduct is not available for cultivation of fruit or vegetables, nor for the sheep and dairy farming that is well established in this area of west Devon. The pink hue of the stone adds a useful splash of colour to contrast with the imposing greens of summer.

Above: Blachford Viaduct: front locomotive GWR 4900 Class 'Hall' 4-6-0 4965 *Rood Ashton Hall*; second locomotive GWR 4073 Class 'Castle' 4-6-0 5043 *Earl of Mount Edgcumbe*, 15 May 2010.

We capture the train as it crosses the viaduct with 'The Cornishman' Vintage Trains railtour which had departed at 16.30 from Plymouth and is bound for Birmingham Snow Hill, hauled by steam to Bristol Temple Meads. The viaduct lies beyond the steeply graded Hemerdon Bank and the ruling gradient is helpfully gentler at this point. The 'Devon duo' of paired locomotives are clearly embracing the opportunity to gain speed and the trail of steam just manages to clear the tailing carriages. It has often been taken for granted by railway photographers that such impressive scenes could recur as and when the railtour charter groups provided them, but during the lockdown times of the COVID-19 virus pandemic they all but vanished and suddenly these scenes became a feature of the past. Fortunately, a few tentative outings featuring steam have facilitated the return of such splendid steam scenes – thus helping to regain such familiarity.

Opposite above: Venton: Class 20s 20205 and 20189 top and tail the 11.40 Plymouth to Derby returning north with a promotional three coach empty stock movement, 20 August 2020.

Class 20s were never part of the far south-west rail scene in BR days and any appearance of these modern day survivors in this region even now is rare. A previous month's light engine pairing of Class 20s also operated by Loram Rail Operations certainly raised a few eyebrows and this was the second appearance of a train operated by the company in Devon. Loram is involved in rolling stock and track infrastructure maintenance, traction training and rolling stock movements for private operators. The Class 20s' authentic BR blue livery certainly appeals and recalls the locomotive's heyday in the 1970s, and the livery applied to the coaching stock certainly catches the eye. Here the train descends towards Totnes and passes a field occasionally occupied by cows, though they were not present to admire the passing ensemble on this occasion.

Below: Hollicombe: First Great Western Class 153 153370 leads an unidentified Class 150, both in Wessex Trains promotional livery and operating the 16.05 Exmouth to Paignton service as it nears its destination, 16 July 2006.

Glorious Devon! The lush green grass and trees suggest there is ample rain around these parts during the summer season. It's a view awaiting a visit to the red sandstone cliffs, coves and beaches by train and already the day trippers and holidaymakers seem to have left the water's edge in order to return to their homes or either bed and breakfast or caravan parks for tea. It sums up the Riviera experience that the founding railway companies wished to promote. Little did they realise that the family car would eventually take away much of their trade while cluttering the local byways and highways with long traffic queues. Now railway booking sites such as Great Western tell you how much C02 emissions you have saved by travelling by train and not by car. Signs of a more environment-friendly appeal are surely to be encouraged.

Teignmouth Sprey Point: Class 47 47747 in Virgin Trains livery heads the 09.13 Liverpool Lime Street to Plymouth, 24 July 2001.

With a glimpse of South Devon's fine sandy beaches and gently rolling waves lapping at their edge, passengers arriving from some inland residences could be forgiven for thinking that they had indeed arrived in some kind of earthly paradise – and the Great Western Railway (GWR) was not cautious in promoting its appeal. The red sandstone cliffs however betray a different story. Global climate change means wetter winters and more frequency of Atlantic storms. This has meant that the cliffs, consisting of a rock which easily crumbles, have been significantly eroded while also having absorbed much more water than previously, acting as a great sponge. This has the consequence of a much increased risk of subsidence and landslides onto the railway. The whole cliff is vulnerable and unstable, and it could easily move and create one huge landslip. Structural enhancements have been deployed in its treatment but it is an ongoing problem which has meant that alternative inland routes have been considered, and now the proposal is to realign the coastal walkway and build the sea wall to a higher level. This means that the railway is moved away from the most hazardous section of the cliffs. Included would be space provided for buttresses to be installed to help stabilise those cliffs judged most vulnerable to landslip. At the time of writing, this is still in the balance as there are local objections to the details concerning such changes to the Teignmouth sea wall. Sprey Point itself was created by Brunel in the mid-1840s to enable materials to be brought directly by boat to the construction site of the South Devon Railway.

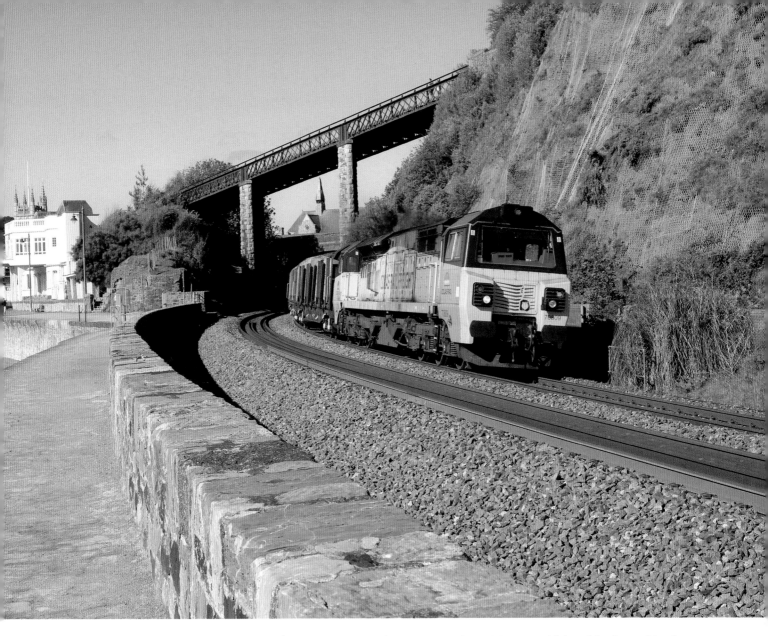

Teignmouth: COLAS Class 70 70809 hauls stored timber wagons from Newton Abbot Hackney Yard to Carlisle, 30 July 2020.

There was a weekly train of timber which operated from the timber sidings at Teigngrace, on the old Moretonhampstead branch, to Chirk during the years 2012 to 2015. It proved a novelty both for reintroducing trains on the long-disused branch – now lifted beyond Heathfield – and for the use of Colas Class 56 locomotives which were something of a novelty to the south-west. This occasion was therefore an unusual train movement, and captures the train as it rounds the curve onto the sea wall after passing through Teignmouth station. On this warm summer's day, the sea wall will soon become busy with walkers and those accessing the beach, although at this early stage of the morning it is mainly the joggers that will keep the sea wall busy, alongside the busy schedule of passing trains.

Teignmouth: A nine-car Class 802 passes the east end of the promenade as it enters along the sea wall with the 07.10 Penzance to London Paddington, 30 July 2020.

These new trains have revolutionised travel on the Berks and Hants route to London Paddington. They operate in diesel mode as far as Newbury where they raise their pantograph for collecting power from the wires onwards to Paddington. At this point a distinctive hum replaces the throb of the diesel motors. Some criticism has been passed on their seating comfort, but the author finds it adequate even for long journeys. They certainly create an impression of sleek modernity here as they start to encounter the red sandstone cliffs which have received significant remedial attention in recent years, in order to buttress them and prevent them from collapsing onto the line and the beach below. The pier and church add atmosphere to the esplanade and lucky sunbathers are promised a fine roast to lobster red in the strong sunlight. Then they will match the red sandstone pictured.

Teignmouth: A nine-car IET Class 802 passes along the sea wall with the 07.04 London Paddington to Paignton, 30 July 2020.

The full sweep of the beach is evident here, and we have Brunel to thank for the fine views along the coast and out to sea as seen by the passengers travelling on board this train. He had not intended this scenic splendour as a benefit purely for gazing at by those travelling on his railway, but rather as a way of accommodating his atmospheric trains which, like these new trains, ran silently and with fast acceleration. The train will already have passed the engine house at Starcross which housed the engines and boilers needed to create the necessary atmospheric pressure. The running costs of this system, apart from those caused by cliff falls and sea-wall breaches, were very high. For example, there was a need for 'greasers' to walk up and down the line smearing grease on the leather valves to keep them supple. Of course the whole section of line from Teignmouth to Dawlish Warren continues to require substantial upkeep, especially after the breach of the sea wall in February 2014 which destroyed part of the line and nearby property just west of Dawlish station. As the author writes there is a much-required remodelling of the sea wall at Dawlish to help deflect waves – which hopefully will enable such views to be enjoyed by many more generations.

Dawlish: Class 40 40145 *East Lancashire Railway*, preserved by the Class 40 Preservation Society, passes at speed with Pathfinder Tours' 'The Cornish Explorer' Penzance to Portsmouth Harbour return excursion, 27 June 2009.

The famed black swans of Dawlish meet, at least in the pictures on the poles, with the railway that is hugging the coastline as it passes along the sea wall. At this seaside resort, it is necessary to cross under or over the railway to reach the beach, thus ensuring that its presence is firmly established in each visitor's holiday memories. The allure of interest in railways for the author started with annual family summer holiday visits to Dawlish, at a time when Class 52 'Western' hauled motorail trains (conveying passengers in coaches attached to car-carrier wagons) fitted in with local diesel multiple units and long-distance passenger and mail trains in an ongoing procession in either direction. On a 1970s summer Saturday, an enquiry at the Dawlish ticket office as to whether the trains were running on time was met with the response, 'It's a summer Saturday and all in the hands of the gods!' This all reflected the vastly increased level of summer Saturday traffic as passengers both arrived at and returned from their holidays at the various coastal resorts of Devon and Cornwall. Indeed it should be recalled that historically across the country, without the railways the seaside holiday would not have been possible for the mass of working class people who were reliant on public transport to reach their seaside destinations and especially so prior to the establishment of motorways and coaches which later facilitated competition. The Class 40 locomotives would have played no part in the 1970s' Western Region scene, dominated by the presence of the hydraulic diesels, and yet they belonged firmly to that 'BR blue era'. Here 40145 *East Lancashire Railway* evokes an appropriate reminder from that past when locomotive-hauled trains were principally features of the long-distance railway journey.

Dawlish: A Great Western Class 802 passes alongside a rough sea with an early afternoon service to London, 23 March 2020.

Vivid spring light accompanies the turbulent sea's lively waves lapping the sea wall on a day when not all is as it seems. The train is operating one of the emergency timetable services introduced just hours before the start of the lockdown that was imposed to slow the transmission of the COVID-19 virus. The atmosphere of the sea therefore reflects the upheaval that was taking place as the health scare dramatically increased its grip on all parts of the country. A very cool easterly wind combined with concerns about health meant that very few people were actually walking along the sea wall that day. The red sandstone cliffs pay their own form of tribute.

Opposite above and below: Cockwood Harbour: BR Standard Class 8P 4-6-2 71000 *Duke of Gloucester* crosses the causeway hauling the 16.42 Kingswear to Bristol 'Torbay Express', 25 July 2010.

With panache and flair this elegant locomotive, truly a giant of steam, encounters the calm waters of the causeway over this inlet from the River Exe estuary as it conveys an expression of the grandeur of BR's epitome of steam locomotive designs. Fitted with Caprotti valve gear, this was the only example of its class to be built. The impressive sounds of the hiss and chuff of the approaching train, along with a clear whistle, must be imagined, and yet we are unavoidably captivated by its very presence. Long after the train has passed will the atmosphere and sense of 'special' linger in the soul of the beholder.

Opposite below: Cockwood Harbour: A Virgin Cross-Country Class 221 Super Voyager operates the 15.25 Plymouth to York, 22 July 2007.

The Virgin Trains livery adds a balance of colour to a typical summer's day scene, with the heat causing a build up of clouds over the land while the estuary remains in dazzling light. A plethora of small boats await the incoming tide and, for some, their worn paintwork speaks of journeys into waters less calm than offered in this cosy inlet. Dare the owners of the glossily-painted boats venture to take them out into the beckoning incoming tide where they might also lose their sheen?

Above: Cockwood Harbour: A First Great Western Class 158 is seen on a mid-pm Exeter St Davids to Penzance service. This unit is in TransPennine Express livery as it was previously based at Leeds, 22 July 2007.

Incongruous as it may seem, this train has many times seen the snows and mists of the peat bogs on its journeys over the TransPennine routes from Leeds to Liverpool. How welcoming it must find the changing gentle hues of the Exe estuary and the warm sandy beaches of the South Devon coast along its new paths. Those visiting holidaymakers, who are travelling from Yorkshire and Lancashire, may not care that it is a livery with which they are familiar, but they certainly share the wonder for the picturesque quays and harbours through which it journeys.

Opposite above: Starcross: Pacers Class 143 143603 and a Class 142 in First Great Western livery depart with the 18.26 Exeter to Paignton, 27 June 2009.

Gazing out of the window towards the water, passengers will note the Exmouth ferry which traverses the Exe estuary towards its meeting with the sea. The captain will need dexterity in steering the vessel between the myriad other sailing vessels which provide an intriguing maze though which to thread a safe path. Much of a pleasure on a fine summer's day, the choppy ride in less favourable conditions will necessitate finding your sealegs.

These Pacer units were diagrammed for such stopping services along the Devon coast. In contrast, it is bizarre to think that one of the lengthy nine-car IET Class 802 units, forming the 17.36 from London Paddington, calls at *all* stations from Exeter St Davids to Paignton, including Exeter St Thomas, Starcross and Dawlish Warren – all made possible with selective door opening, though passengers intending to depart such trains will need clear messaging about which carriage to sit in.

Below: Exeter St Davids: paired South West Trains Class 159s, with 159010 in Stagecoach livery at the rear, depart with the 18.10 to London Waterloo, 27 June 2009.

Canopies and latticework footbridges, red brickwork and painted columns, all accompanied by traditional station furniture such as luggage trolleys and signposts, inspire the main line station with character and personality. Concrete modern platforms and sleepers are part of the modern railway scene, but they hardly exude any atmosphere such as that abundantly evident here at St Davids during a quiet spell after the evening rush hour.

Above: Eggesford: A First Great Western Class 142 Pacer diesel multiple unit leads a Class 143 with the 12.43 ex-Barnstaple, 7 January 2010.

Caught between the long shadows and low winter's day sunlight, we see the up platform station building. It was built by the North Devon Railway in August 1854 and later transferred to the LSWR. It is a double-fronted asymmetrical building of restrained Tudor Gothic style, with the south-west front facing the platform. A grand and imposing building for a location which is two and a half miles from the nearest village at Chulmleigh, it stands as a proud and homely tribute to the original railway company. Passengers would arrive courtesy of the local horse-drawn carriage, and some might be heading to the hustle and bustle of the city of Exeter. Their peace and calm, however, remains fully respected here as the day's sunlight slowly starts to fade on this rural reflection as it contemplates the onset of a particularly cold night .

Opposite above: Lymington River Bridge: 3CIG Class 421 unit 1497 in heritage BR blue and grey livery heads toward Lymington Pier with an early evening service, 9 September 2006.

A timely reminder of the days of BR Southern Region with its classic electric multiple units, this version has more spacious seating and is here running in authentic 'heritage' BR blue and grey livery. By this date all other slam door suburban stock had been withdrawn but special dispensation was granted to South West Trains for the Class 421 units to continue in service along the five and a half mile branch line from Brockenhurst to Lymington Pier. The busy moorings with their leisure and fishing vessels hint at the nearby sea with its views towards the Isle of Wight. The scene could as well have appeared exactly the same thirty years previously.

Below: Richmond: Class 378 'CapitalStar' electric multiple units 013 and 017 await duties in providing services on the North London line section of the London Overground system. A London Transport District line train awaits passengers at the far right, 5 June 2010.

Aesthetic aspects of train design have not always been given a priority during the era of modern railways, both within the UK and in Western Europe. Several designs in the twenty-first century have suggested that a turning point has been passed, whereby the appearance of the train is recognised as having value, more than being simply functional. While a focus on 'making an impression' has been prioritised for high speed trains, there have also been efforts to present suburban train fleets with more visual appeal. These 'CapitalStar' Class trains were new to service in July 2009 and still look new to service as seen here a year later. Their cab design looks smart and neat, tidy and more rounded than the sharp, blunt lines of previous modern designs. The livery promotes the impact of company colours for effect (including for such purpose as indicating the location of doors) in such a way that it complements and synthesises with the contours of the shape of the train. The interior longitudinal seating and high capacity for standing passengers corresponded with a vast increase in passengers travelling on the orbital London Overground network for which they were designed. Clearly the travelling public were attracted to the travel experience offered on these new trains. The presence of a District Line train reinforces the metropolitan atmosphere of the station, accompanied by some rather fine wrought iron canopy brackets.

Above: Richmond Bridge: A South West Trains Class 450 crosses the Thames with Richmond in the background lit by early spring afternoon sunshine, 11 March 2020.

The Georgian houses of Richmond's Thames waterfront bask in the sunshine and their calm atmosphere is echoed by the calm waters of the river. The arches of the bridge are equally in harmony as they pay their own graceful tribute to the waterside scene. The amber leaves of the trees – almost autumnal in hue yet actually in full spring flourish – complement the freshly-applied vivid blue and orange livery carried by this South Western Railway service. Rather like nature as it emerges from winter to spring, all the movement here represents a rhythm responding to the late afternoon's fleeting light as twilight draws on.

Opposite: London St Pancras station: view south towards the clock, with an overview of the undercroft and new openings through existing blind arches in the west wall, 8 April 2008.

In this unrivalled architectural gem of Victorian Gothic, the merging of the modern St Pancras's requirements such as the lift and digital information screens with the traditional features of this masterpiece is accomplished with exceptional eloquence and aplomb. The uplifting curvature of the cast iron arches of the canopy recalls the brush strokes of an accomplished artist attempting to convey the sense of an upward sweep in our gaze towards the brightly lit iron and glass roof which, at the time of its construction, was the largest single span roof in the world. It measures 240m long, spans 75m and is 30m high. The distinctive red midland brickwork from Nottingham, painstakingly cleaned and restored, appears to rest on the very pillars supporting the walkway over the undercroft's cafes and shops. The dressed stone is carved by hand. Natural light is dispersed through the 11,000 panes of glass in the canopy to even this low-level promenade, bypassed by thousands of passengers each day and previously a mere beer barrel storage area below the platforms, facilitates the airy atmosphere of this grand tribute to the Midland Railway. Like any great Gothic cathedral, in this railway cathedral can be found many intricate features which combine to aid contemplation and worship – albeit secular – of such magnificent architecture. Surely this immense splendour could be a pointer to that great Creator and Designer who inspires such human achievement?

London St Pancras: Eurostar Class 373 sets (3218 on far right) at rest in the Eurostar terminal platforms, early afternoon, 25 August 2009.

As often happens, that which is perceived as standard and everyday soon becomes historic and interesting when fleets of trains are replaced, as have the majority of these trendsetters in terms of very high speed trains to and within Europe (running at up to 186mph in daily service). They reached as far as Marseille in ordinary service and operated some of the French ski destination trains in peak season. Three of the Regional Eurostar units were leased by the Great North Eastern Railway (GNER) to enhance services between London King's Cross, York and Leeds. Many consider these soundly-constructed original Eurostar trains as 'gone with some regret' as their much newer replacements have a reputation for a bouncy ride in certain places, on the route to Paris at least, and the author can verify this. They have certainly earned their keep and Eurostar donated a power car to the National Railway Museum – a genuine honour in tribute of their achievement and place in UK railway history. The subtle shadows highlight the distinctive cabs of these admirable ambassadors. The principal trusses within the wrought ironwork, so clearly evident here in its full sweep of the train shed, are a product of the Butterley Iron Company of Derby. Along with the brickwork, St Pancras is very much a showpiece by the Midland Railway for what the company could transport from the Midlands to the capital and beyond.

London Liverpool Street station: between duties, Class 86 86215 in ex-works Anglia Railways livery alongside Class 86 86223 *Norwich Union* in InterCity livery, 12 September 1998.

A cool £120 million was spent redeveloping this station between 1985 and 1991, and it shows! Liverpool Street was originally formed of two separate areas known as the Eastern train shed and the Western train shed. During the redevelopment the Eastern shed was demolished and the original Western shed carefully restored. The wrought iron columns, glass roof and intricate metalwork supporting the canopy along with the renewed platform surfaces all combine to support yet another accolade award as 'railway cathedral' for this magnificent building, and the brightly lit and airy atmosphere is a far cry from its previous dingy, unkempt state. Class 86 locomotives, having proved reliable and efficient workhorses on the West Coast main line, adapted well to use on the East Anglian main line services to Ipswich and Norwich. Their presence complements the grandiose surroundings to which they pay tribute.

Above: Wandsworth Road, viewed towards Battersea Power Station: Eurostar Class 373 373215 leads, 373216 at rear, 12.27 London Waterloo to Brussels Midi, 3 April 1996.

The modern railway scene includes trains which once were the height of quality and innovation yet are now nearly completely replaced by newer and sleeker trains – although often with a less impressive ride! This Eurostar train represented a vast technological advance in rail travel as it attained speeds far higher than any previously experienced on UK rails during its journey to and through the Channel Tunnel, and especially within France on its roller-coaster route paralleling the motorways to Paris. It was scintillating and exciting to simply glide past any traffic on the roads and leave *all* behind in its quest for speed. In contrast, at the time of this photograph, the new trains departed from London Waterloo and had to painfully crawl along the slower suburban lines of South London while negotiating the various complex junctions until reaching the dedicated high speed route in Kent. St Pancras International, which has since 2007 replaced Waterloo, enjoys the benefits of a fast line throughout to the tunnel and thence the European continent.

Opposite above: Purley Oaks: front locomotive Class 73 73136 *Kent Youth Music* in Mainline blue livery and, at rear, Class 73 73131 in EWS livery, haul the 16.30 Willesden to Dover Travelling Post Office (TPO), 16 April 2003.

This TPO train was routed via Redhill and Tonbridge Royal Mail depot to Dover. It provided a refreshing splash of colour to the local scene while at the same time, as it was locomotive hauled, it broke the relative monotony of the familiar diet of electric multiple units on the Southern Region main line. It is, as ever, gone with regret, and no doubt its replacement giant lorries enjoy the dubious benefits of navigating the M25 with their important loads being delayed in its permanent road congestion. These trains were always a welcome sight across the network and this particular one was in its final days of glory for it would be withdrawn from operation in July 2003.

Below: Norwich: a mid-evening view with, on the left, a National Express East Anglia Class 90 and on the right is EWS Class 90 90028 on loan, 30 May 2008.

The fading sunlight reinforces the indication that these locomotives appear intent on completing their forthcoming journeys to London before nightfall, though such is deceitful for one of them is only going to the stabling point with empty coaching stock for servicing. The angular thrust of the Class 90 locomotive cab certainly conveys a message of forward movement and the overhead wires are less intrusive than at some locations, helping to keep the viewer's gaze firmly on the locomotives in their contrasting liveries. The fleet of twelve-car Class 745 'Flirt' units (built by Stadler) delivered to Greater Anglia for services to London during 2019 and 2020 has effectively sealed the departure of these locomotives from the East Anglia main line scene.

Above: Wymondham: National Express East Anglia Class 170 Turbostar 170272 in Anglia Railways livery arrives with the 10.15 service to Norwich, 29 May 2008.

The modern UK railway has several local stations which merge their provision of the most updated facilities with respect for upholding the heritage atmosphere, such as here at Wymondham. With features reflected in the preservation scene, we see fire buckets, floral displays, a door canopy, semaphore and ground signals and a characteristic footbridge, all of which combine to backtrack in their welcome given to the passengers in the arriving train as well as to the awaiting suited gentleman who appears to gesture towards the train as it slows for its stop. It recalls a typical summer's day scene from the 1960s and is not compromised by the sleek new diesel unit – which intriguingly blends in very well.

Opposite above: Ely Marina: An EWS Class 66 hauls an early afternoon north-bound Lafarge stone train from Kennet Redland Sidings to Mount Sorrel, 28 May 2008.

The Great Ouse River flows past the Fenland city of Ely and is crossed by a busy through-route for freight trains as well as frequent passenger trains. The canal boats find safe moorings and the spring sunshine breaks through to give its welcome warmth to this pastoral scene. All is calm preceding the arrival of the heavy stone train which rumbles across the bridge and into the distance, after which the quiet returns until the next arrival disturbs the swans.

Opposite below: Near Ely by the Great Ouse River: A Central Trains/Cross-Country Class 170/1 or 170/5 two-car Turbostar passes with a midday service from Birmingham to Leicester and Stansted Airport. The livery is Central Trains with CrossCountry silver vinyls, 28 May 2008.

Fenland may be flat, but the long lush grass provides plenty of delicious grazing and a comfortable location to view the passing trains in between milking times, if you are a bovine enjoying a rest and need something to pass the time of day. Quite what she thinks about the procession of trains we shall never know, though writing down any numbers is out of the question and keeping a track of which one goes where is best left to those strange people who come along occasionally consulting those mobile phone things – and it's best to ignore that photographer chap behind …

Cardiff Central: at left is Advenza Freight Class 57/0 57005 (ex-47350) based at Gloucester but stored at Cardiff Central, stabled. To its right is Advenza Freight Class 66/8 66842 (previously 66407, renumbered April 2009) based at Gloucester, also stabled, 26 September 2009.

How things change! By the time this photograph was taken, these locomotives were virtually history. They were used on Stockton and Shipley to Cardiff Tidal scrap metal trains. They were also used to provide haulage for out-of-course movements of rolling stock to storage points and workshops. Advenza Freight was the shortest lived of the freight companies to use Class 66. It was a subsidiary of Cotswold Rail (which itself commenced operation in 2006), commencing use of four Class 66/8 in summer 2009 when taking over off-lease Direct Rail Services (DRS) locomotives. The locomotives were quickly painted in Advenza Freight livery but after amassing significant debts the company was taken into receivership in early October 2009, Network Rail having suspended their contract on 6 October 2009. The locomotives returned to the lease owner (Porterbrook). Declines in quantities of metals and construction traffic in recent years meant that expansion of rail traffic was unavailable to this new firm.

The 'Sleeperz' sign above the accommodation behind the locomotives *could* be considered a play on words for those cognisant in rail terminology, for whom 'Sleepers' could refer to 'sleeper trains' (the nearest to Cardiff work from Penzance to London Paddington) or to the sleepers on which the rails are laid.

Birmingham New Street: London Midland Class 323 three-car electric multiple unit 323215 departs with the 13.37 service to Wolverhampton (ex-Walsall), 4 August 2008.

The renowned gloom of Birmingham New Street is dispelled both by the summer's day rays of light and, away from the depths of the station interior, this attractive green livery which adds an almost rustic flavour to alleviate the impact of the imposing city offices which stand as sentries to the exit of the station. This smart looking electric unit providing a local stopping service makes a bid for the gloom of the tunnels which eventually permit an escape to the open vistas lying beyond. The mix of styles in the various surrounding buildings further helps to add to the tapestry of the busy city station.

Venetian Marina Ltd and Wardle Canal Moorings: An Arriva Trains Wales Class 158 passes by, operating the 09.28 from Holyhead, 11.14 Chester to Crewe. The Wardle Canal forms a branch off the nearby Shropshire Union Canal, 26 October 2006.

This picture combines two photographic subjects that are favourites of mine – railways and canals. The former essentially replaced the latter as a quicker and more effective mode of transport for carrying goods and the travelling public, whereas the latter has developed to facilitate a mainly leisure pursuit – with some people more than happy to make a lengthy canal narrow-boat into their home. Such boats pose no limits for gardeners, for I have seen them used virtually as greenhouses, with flourishing home-grown vegetables and bountiful floral displays. The attractive colours given to canal boats, often personalised by boat owners or smartly branded by canal boat hire companies, help give them an identity and character – which is less than can be said about the rather ordinary livery carried by this diesel unit. So there's a lesson that at least some of the railway companies can learn from their 'competitors' on the canals. Mind you it's a dramatic sky, which bodes stormy weather ahead when there will be a need to 'batten down the hatches'.

Bangor: Class 31/4 31465 in Regional Railways livery arrives with empty coaching stock for the 10.30 Saturdays-only Bangor to Manchester Piccadilly (normally to Manchester Victoria but the route was not available owing to engineering works on this date), 14 August 1993.

'Regional Railways' was an epithet which didn't quite summarise the nature of the services that were offered under its umbrella of routes which were essentially secondary to the higher standards of the main line. However, it provided a fortunate experience for those interested in unusual locomotive haulage along such routes as the North Wales line which passed some scenic byways on its route from Chester to Bangor and Holyhead. Vintage locomotives ruled the roost with summer Saturday services and, when loaded passenger trains required additional carriages, stock such as this was made available as it was not required for rush-hour commuters. Provision of adequate seats for 'passengers' was seen as important. In later times, 'customers' had to put up with short crowd-crushed, bus-seated 'Pacers' without additional carriages being supplied (such carriages had, by then, all been withdrawn). This scene captures the eclectic mix of a traditional signal box and locomotive-hauled carriages, accompanied by somewhat incongruous modern electric signalling.

Above: Holyhead: Class 37/4s with, at right, 37418 fitted with snow ploughs and in Railfreight Petroleum livery ready to attach to the coaching stock of the 16.00 to Crewe; at left is 37421, also fitted with snow ploughs and in Railfreight Petroleum livery, moving its empty coaching stock for the 14.30 Holyhead to Crewe to the front end of the departure platform, 14 August 1993.

The presence of a Stena Line ship berthed here at Holyhead indicates that there is a crowd of passengers who will descend to the platform for the next available services for Manchester, Liverpool and all points beyond Chester and Crewe. Little will they care for the fact that they will be hauled by freight locomotives which have been requisitioned for the means of conveying their carriages on a summer Saturday when everyone, it seems, is on the move. Those rail enthusiasts present, however, could hardly believe their luck in finding two such examples providing the necessary motive power. It was rather like a rail enthusiasts' fiesta but without the hoards of enthusiasts being present – perhaps there were similar distractions elsewhere in the north-west on this day? Certainly the number of camera-toting aficionados present was far fewer than if this spectacle was to occur today. The loud and exhilarating scream of the Class 37 engines continues to appeal to modern enthusiasts and their reliability and flexibility have proved very popular both within the private sector and with heritage railways.

Opposite above: Liverpool Lime Street Station: London Midland Class 350/1 Desiro electric multiple unit 350123 awaits departure with the 08.40 service to Birmingham New Street, 8 August 2008.

The elliptical curvature of the train roof mirrors that of the splendid arches of Lime Street's historic train shed, all of which is amply lit by the acres of glass canopy and by the Victorian arched gable end at the main entrance to the station terminus. The mottled effect of interlaced light and shadow reinforces the intricacy of the arched metalwork, which is no doubt kept clean through meticulous cleaning and repainting by a dedicated team of specialists whose efforts are indeed praiseworthy. The empty taxi roadway suggests that the London service has long since departed, and adds to the somewhat deserted atmosphere that pervades – after all, the crowds of inbound commuters will have already hastened to their places of work, oblivious to the finesse of this architectural jewel.

Below: Warrington 'Twelve Arches': EWS Class 66 66218 departs Arpley Yard at Walton Old Junction with a train of empty coal wagons from Fiddlers Ferry, 5 August 2005.

Here the River Mersey is crossed by an attractive sandstone viaduct which carries the short avoiding line that links into Arpley & Walton sidings and where the west coast main line viaduct crosses the river Mersey behind. The train is en route for Walton Old Junction Sidings and ultimately for Liverpool Bulk Terminal. At this point, the river is tidal and has been subject to a vast clean up, with seals apparently having been seen as far upstream as Warrington.

Blackpool North: A First TransPennine Express Desiro Class 185 passes Blackpool North No. 2 signal box and semaphore signals with a train from Manchester, 11 April 2010.

The station staff at Blackpool North had a notorious reputation for hounding off the platforms anyone who vaguely attempted to take photographs or fitted into the 'train-spotter' category. There were regular letters of complaint to the railway media magazines. Yet here on a springtime Sunday I was entirely unhindered – indeed there seemed to be no staff around (Sunday shifts are often unpopular). Fifteen semaphore signals can be counted. All this would change completely within the next decade, when the traditional signalling and signal box was decommissioned on 11 November and the box was demolished on 14–15 November 2017, after which the line between Preston and the two Blackpool stations was closed for resignalling and electrification to Blackpool North.

Lancaster Station: DB Schenker Class 92 92017 *Bart the Engine*, in Stobart Rail livery, approaches with the 06.25 Rugby to Mossend Tesco container train, 14 April 2010.

Privatisation of the railways has certainly encouraged opportunities to promote advertising and 'alternative' liveries to those of the standard company colours. This is seen to full effect here and its flare complements the longer sweep of the Class 92 body, especially the white surround that is applied to the cab. A sense of speed and motion is well conveyed – indeed the train passes at speed here on dedicated through-lines. Stobart's lorries are part of folklore on the northern motorways as they ply their way to and from Scotland, and it is pleasing to see this environment-friendly use made of rail in reliable, daily operated services. You can set your watch by their timekeeping, as compared to that of the trucks stuck in the endless quagmire of roadworks and motorway-upgrading with their associated miles of queuing traffic and ever-frustrated drivers.

Lancaster station: Virgin Trains Class 390 'Pendolino' tilting electric train 390011 operating the 09.55 Lancaster, ex-London Euston, to Glasgow Central, 16 April 2010.

These are impressive trains, with their Fiat Ferroviaria tilting system and the sleek and curvaceous sweep of the front cab is enhanced by such a stylish livery . They ascend the heavy gradient encountered on the southern approach to Shap as if it is a mere inconvenience, and glide around sharp curves giving an impression of steadiness and confidence. A trip on one of these from Lancaster to Carlisle will be a feast for the eyes as the train passes the grandiose mountains of Lakeland, and the train seeks to accompany such grandeur in its own inimitable style while whisking its passengers in comfort and warmth as they gaze on the unfolding natural beauty of the fells. Once over the Scottish border, the surge of power is again impressive as it ascends the climb up Beattock, almost as if it is a racehorse grasping at the tether. Who says that modern rail engineering lacks character?

Lancaster Station: Class 325 Postal electric multiple units in Royal Mail livery are seen operating a southbound service from Shieldmuir Mail Terminal to Warrington Royal Mail or Willesden Mail Terminal, 16 April 2010.

In tribute to the opening lines of W.H. Auden's 'Night Mail' to the 1936 GPO documentary film about the work of the TPO, it would not quite ring so authentically for this multiple unit train by saying, 'Here comes the daytime mail having earlier crossed the Border, Bringing the email and the BACS payment order', but at least it *is* a mail train – for most of such traffic was lost after January 2004 when the last TPO services made their final journeys. The livery recalls that of the Rail Express Systems fleet and the service acknowledges the fact that there is still value in sending 'mail by rail'. No doubt some of those parcels being conveyed will be distributed by the flourishing Amazon, and parcel delivery vans will be seen buzzing around our cities and rural destinations.

Above: Lancaster station: Class A1 4-6-2 60163 *Tornado* hauls the 09.00 'The Cumbrian Coast Tornado' (originating at Crewe) excursion from Preston to Carlisle via the Cumbrian Coast, operated by HF Railtours, 14 April 2010.

It is interesting to note that the newest thing to be seen in this photograph is the locomotive! Gleaming and sparkling in the spring sunshine, it always draws attention as an intentional tribute to the expression of British steam locomotive engineering at its best. Completed in 2008 in Darlington, it was built to the design detail of the Peppercorn development of Thompson's Class A1 Pacific. The original class was built between 1948 and 1949. Ever popular, it has covered over 100,000 miles and seen service on the Network Rail main line and heritage railways right across Great Britain. It needed some substantial repairs in 2018.

The main station building, in Tudor Revival style using roughly squared sandstone and constructed in 1846 by William Tite, is situated on the west side of the main line. The two-storey building was extended southwards in 1852 and terminates in a tower of three storeys at the south end.

Opposite above: Arnside Viaduct: First TransPennine Siemens Desiro Class 185 185106 (introduced to service 13 January 2006) crosses the viaduct over the River Kent estuary with the 15.27 Manchester Airport to Barrow-in-Furness service, 1 June 2007.

This fifty-one span viaduct with its fifty piers commands a fine view over the Kent estuary which flows into Morecambe Bay. It is viewed equally well from the promenade at Arnside as well as from Arnside Knott, which rewards any climb up on a clear day, affording views over the eye-catching viaduct and the surrounding countryside. Such a vista includes Whitbarrow Scar and South Lakeland.

Below: Arnside Viaduct: A Northern Trains Class 153 with an afternoon service from Lancaster to Barrow-in-Furness crosses over the River Kent estuary, 6 August 2005.

At high tide the waters of the estuary envelope the viaduct, and the tide rises and falls very quickly, as it also does in Morecambe Bay. This makes the waters of the bay treacherous and any attempt to cross must only be done with an experienced guide and following a particular route. There is a legend that tells of the tide's inrush as being faster than that which an expert horse-rider can gallop.

Above: Arnside Viaduct: A Northern Trains Class 156 with an early afternoon service from Barrow-in-Furness to Lancaster crossing over River Kent estuary, 1 June 2007.

There is certainly a contrast here between the rather gaudy metallic aquamarine livery carried by the diesel unit and the natural tidal blue of the estuary waters. Prominent also is the red of the upper quadrant semaphore signal in the 'off' position which draws attention both to the arriving train and to the mottled green of the surrounding hills. The fleeting sun has broken through the clouds at just the right time to illuminate the train's appearance and bathes the viaduct in a light which accentuates the colour of the red brick and shadows cast below. Such is not always the railway photographer's luck and many a time those clouds would have arrived just in time to cast a suppressed shadow over all that looks so attractive in the sunlight.

Opposite: Near Grange-over-Sands: A First TransPennine Express Siemens Desiro Class 185 passes the salt marshes and sandbanks of the River Kent estuary, as it approaches with the 11.00 Manchester Airport to Barrow-in-Furness service, 13 August 2009.

Here we see Arnside Knott in the background (righthand side) with its dominant position alongside the estuary. There is a salute provided by both semaphore signals – always a welcome aspect of railway heritage, giving character to the scene in their own way – as they pay tribute to the passing express diesel unit. The roster of Class 185 units for use on this route, with their appealing design both in passenger comfort and appearance, enhanced with First TransPennine Express 'Dynamic Lines' livery, improved significantly the quality of trains provided for the Manchester to Barrow route. By 2019 these had all but disappeared from this branch line, being requisitioned for much-needed increased frequency of services over the Pennines, and their additional comfort and spacious interiors no doubt were much missed by commuters and long-distance visitors alike. Fortunately for them, the pastoral landscape of this Lakeland region remains unchanged and continues to be enjoyed by the many visitors to the small towns along the route.

Above: Grange-over-Sands: First TransPennine Express Siemens Desiro Class 185 185148 in First TransPennine Express 'Dynamic Lines' livery approaches the station with the 09.00 Manchester Airport to Barrow-in-Furness service, Thursday 13 August 2009.

On the left-hand side in the down direction, this train passes the salt marshes and sandbanks of the River Kent estuary and Morecambe Bay. The proximity of the position of the estuarine channel determines how close the sea actually comes to the sea wall. As it moves eastwards, saltmarsh growth along the seafront becomes established whereas when the channel moves westwards, the marsh becomes eroded accompanied by a lowering of the foreshore. Back in the 1970s I recall the water lapping at the sea wall here at Grange whereas at the time of this visit there were sheep grazing in well established grasses in the marshes. The well preserved station, extensively restored in the late 1990s, remains a more stable reminder of the Furness Railway Company who rebuilt it c. 1877. Note on the right the Furness Railway goods shed, previously an engine shed.

Opposite above: Grange-over-Sands: Northern Trains Class 142 142034 departs with the 12.41 ex- Carlisle via Barrow, 16.03 from Grange-over-Sands to Lancaster, 1 June 2007.

This photograph amply demonstrates the vast marshes which become established when the estuarine channel moves eastward. It's a less familiar location for photographers than that afforded at the Dawlish and Teignmouth sea wall, but reinforces how much the railway is influenced by the cycles of nature and its almost obsequious responses. Arnside Knott can be seen in the centre distance. A stroll up to the top on a fine day is thoroughly commended as it offers stunning views over Arnside viaduct, the River Kent estuary and the surrounding Lakeland scenery. Pity any passengers who have travelled from distant parts of the Cumbrian coast on this 'Pacer' unit with its bus-type body and seating. It would be a roller-coast of a ride – literally!

Opposite below: Ulverston Station: First TransPennine Class 185 185129 departs with the 13.22 Ulverston, 11.27 ex-Manchester Airport to Barrow-in-Furness service, 1 June 2007.

Some stations in Britain have retained a valuable heritage atmosphere, no less so than the Furness Railway platforms at Ulverston. Here in abundance we find attractive glazed canopies on iron supports with the 'FR' emblem evident in the finials, and intricately decorated stairwell railings. It may seem unusual to have platforms at either side of the down line but this arrangement once facilitated transfer onto trains departing for the scenic branch line to Lakeside station at the south end of Windermere, until that was closed to passengers in September 1965. It is always welcome to see such a local station which is evidently cared for and looked after.

Opposite: Ulverston Station: View through the platform canopies, 1 June 2007.

The Furness Railway built this fine station with its red sandstone in 1878. It is a two storey building, Italianate in style, with a French pavilion roof, and flanked by a fine clock tower. The platforms have attractive glazed canopies on iron supports, and the green and reds of the painted metalwork with its finials, railings and Furness Railway insignia echoes the greens and reds of the shrubs and bushes forming a backdrop to the railway architecture. It's a fine example of how our railway heritage can be enhanced by careful restoration and maintenance.

Below: Ravenglass: Class 37/4 37402 passes over Ravenglass Viaduct on the scenic Cumbrian Coast railway with the 14.35 Carlisle to Barrow-in-Furness, 20 April 2018.

It was too good to be true for vintage Class 37 diesel locomotives to be found hauling rakes of coaches along the route from Lancaster to Carlisle via the Cumbrian coast in the latter years of the second decade of the twenty-first century. Yet their distinctive English Electric engines, growling as they drew away from each station halt while attempting to keep up with a timetable intended for short local diesel multiple units, meant that such sounds and sights became a regular event – all thanks to a shortage of trains while new fleets were being built and tested. One can almost hear the full attention being paid by the enthusiasts aboard to such a cacophony of sound, one that could be heard long after the train had departed the frame as the peace returns to this tranquil quayside. Whether the enthusiasts aboard, absorbed by the thrill of their trusty steed's performance, were aware of, or more likely oblivious to, this picturesque scene we can only speculate.

Flimby: DRS Class 47/4 47501 *Craftsman* heads the 14.00 Maryport to Workington road bridge replacement service. DRS Class 57/0 57012 is at rear, Thursday 15 April 2010.

This unusual sight became the norm for a time after the North Workington road bridge over the River Derwent was swept away by torrential rain on 19 November 2009. A seventeen-mile diversion was needed, but the rail distance is half a mile, thus a temporary new two-platform station with a connecting footbridge ('Workington North') was provided by Network Rail near Siddick on the north side of the River Derwent, in order to ease the resulting access problems to the town. This was opened 30 November 2009. With no spare diesel multiple units in the Northern Rail fleet, DRS used three of its Mk 3 coaches redundant from the end of the Stobart Pullman in 2009 and a hired-in Mk 2 from West Coast Railways. The fleet of locomotives included Class 37/4 37423 alongside the Class 47 and 57 featured. DRS provided locomotive crew, guard and stewards. Short platforms fitting two carriages at Flimby and Workington North required the DRS crew to remind passengers to be in the right place to alight. The service was funded by the Department for Transport and was free to use, being available until 2 May 2010.

Plantation Bridge, near Staveley: First TransPennine Express Class 185 185119 operates the
17.06 Windermere to Manchester Airport, 16 April 2010.

Providing a high quality ride for their fortunate passengers on board, these express diesel units were
something of a luxury considering the cautious speed limit along the single branch line serving Kendal
and Windermere, but this one certainly looks snug in the setting of the Lakeland hills – could one even
say that it is 'enjoying the ride'? It will soon stretch its legs in terms of speed once it reaches the West
Coast Main Line and heads for the big city.

Carlisle: DRS Class 66 66434, hired by Colas, hauls the 12.06 Chirk to Carlisle timber empties c. 17.50, and was booked via the West Coast Main Line; the locomotive was previously subleased to Fastline Freight, 13 April 2010.

Some of these railway liveries betray the occasionally rapid changes in the private sector of the UK rail scene, as we saw earlier at Cardiff. The train is operated by Colas and the locomotive, previously subleased to Fastline Freight and in that company's livery, is hired from DRS, having been previously owned by Jarvis Rail Ltd/Fastline Freight which had recently ceased operating freights and gone into administration on 31 March 2010, just prior to this photograph. Colas at this time usually used its own 66s (66841-844, all ex-Advenza). None of the Fastline Class 66s 66301-305 were in use after the time of their withdrawal from freight operations. At the same time as events above, E.ON withdrew its five year £40 million contract with Fastline, making the demise of the operator inevitable. Fastline Freight was formed as a subsidiary of Fastline Ltd, a large supplier of on-track machines and small plant to Network Rail. Fastline Ltd in turn was part of Jarvis plc, acquired in 1997 shortly after rail privatisation. Jarvis saw freight as an attractive addition to its business, already owning a licence to run trains and able to acquire a track access agreement with relative ease. Are you keeping up? Even the experts in the rail business at the time found such pace of change a challenge to follow.

Armathwaite: LMS 'Jubilee' Class 6P 4-6-0 5690 *Leander* accelerates the 'Fellsman' as it climbs south over the Settle and Carlisle Railway with the 15.20 Carlisle to Lancaster via Settle, 12 August 2009.

This train was operated by Statesman Rail Ltd in partnership with Northern Rail and West Coast Railways, and it ran weekly, such was – and is – the appetite for steam on the famous Settle and Carlisle railway, offering its steady climbs and challenging grades. A regular feature was *Leander* which was a Stanier development of the Patriot Class. The LMS maroon fits the location and coaching set very authentically.

The signal box was opened 16 July 1899 and is a standard timber-built 'Midland type 2b' design. It was built (in kit form) at the Midland Railway Company's signalling workshops in Derby, then erected on its current site. It remains owned by Network Rail, but is classed as a 'non-operational heritage asset'. It was leased to the Friends of the Settle Carlisle Line (FoSCL) in 1992 and it has since been fully restored to its Midland Railway appearance (the yellow-and-red paint scheme is authentic).

Above: Kirkby Stephen: Freightliner Class 66/9 66957 *Stephenson Locomotive Society 1909–2009* hauls this southbound Killoch Colliery to Ratcliffe Power Station Freightliner Heavy Haul loaded coal train, passing as scheduled at 16.31, 13 April 2010.

You can stay on holiday here! 'Platform Cottage' shares the finely restored Midland Railway station building with 'Booking Office Cottage' and mutually appeals to rail enthusiasts and fell walkers in the beautiful and unspoilt Upper Eden Valley of Cumbria. Fewer freights now pass, as a result of the switch from power stations' use of coal to biomass (such as Drax power station in North Yorkshire). However, there are still the occasional steam trains, some freight and the regular passenger diesel units to keep you occupied. Keep in mind that it is a half-hour walk down into town followed by similar back up the hill. This is because the railway has to keep height as it ascends towards Ais Gill summit and the Midland Railway's desire to restrict gradients on the line to 1 in 100 meant that the station would necessarily be somewhat remote from the town in the valley.

Opposite above: Approaching Dandry Mire Viaduct: Colas Class 66 66843 approaches, hauling the southbound afternoon Kronospan timber from Carlisle to Chirk, 14 April 2010.

The vast, wild and untamed nature of the Eden district to the south of Kirkby Stephen is clearly evident as this timber train is dwarfed both by the big skies and the surrounding moors and dales. The residents of the few houses in the hamlet located within the Yorkshire Dales National Park no doubt relish the landscape's stark beauty but also must contemplate the full force of the Cumbrian winter or alternatively the steady trudge of adventurous walkers during the summer. For residents and visitors alike, it is an unrivalled location and the train crew clearly have their work cut out as they must control the pull of the train as it threads its way along this magnificent tribute to railway engineering, immersed in the surrounding landscape. We onlookers merely gaze with our own sense of awe.

Below: Approaching Garsdale Station: after crossing Dandry Mire Viaduct, Colas Class 66 66843 hauls the southbound afternoon Kronospan timber from Carlisle to Chirk, 14 April 2010.

This locomotive had previously, as Class 66/4 66408, been operated by DRS and was then overhauled for use by Advenza Freight. Until February of 2010 this service had been hauled by Class 57/3 locomotives hired from DRS. Class 66s were allocated because the timber trains had recently been lengthened to 21 KFA wagons (previously up to 13 KFA wagons) in order to meet increased output from Kielder Forest, and these required a more powerful locomotive. Also at this time, the Class 66/8 was in use down the Settle and Carlisle line as part of a semi-regular operation, as opposed to its previous routing via the West Coast Main Line, in order for Colas to build up driver knowledge for permanent routing over the Settle and Carlisle.

Originally this crossing of Dandry Mire was planned to be an embankment, but when construction started continuous wagon loads of material simply disappeared, swallowed up into the Mire and so a viaduct was built. Construction of this for the Midland Railway Company was a lengthy business and took place from 1869 until 1875. The limestone scar on the hill behind is very typical of the Yorkshire Dales National Park, as also are the dry stone walls.

Garsdale Station: A Northern Class 158 diesel unit departs with the 12.49 Leeds to Carlisle, with the signal box levers clearly in view, 14 April 2010.

How the sunshine brings out the best of this remote location! Regular travellers on the line will know that this is indeed lucky, for the rampaging torrents of rain and heavy snow in early spring can paint a far less welcoming picture. Apart from the smartly liveried diesel unit and grey-painted electrical apparatus box, this scene could have been photographed in the 1960s. It's very much a tribute to the work of the FoSCL, initially formed to actively protest the proposed closure of the line, who have invested much time, effort and money into the buildings, station furniture and gardens of the Settle and Carlisle. The station was restored after a £250,000 refresh thanks to Network Rail and the Railway Heritage Trust. The waiting room of the northbound platform was once used for church services (the famed Settle and Carlisle railway photographer, Bishop Eric Treacy, would surely have approved!) and the ladies' waiting room contained a small library. You can just see the row of levers inside the downside signal box – providing a genuine recollection of many Midland signal boxes built in this style (that at Garsdale was built in 1910). Originally this station was called 'Hawes Junction', and a six-mile line branched off to the Wensleydale town of Hawes.

Garsdale station: DBS Class 66/0 66051 hauls the late-running 12.40 Newbiggin to Milford/Warrington southbound Gypsum train, 14 April 2010.

It is intriguing to note that the line has, during the late twentieth century and first part of the twenty-first, seen significant freight with coal, gypsum and timber all conveyed. Occasional diversions of West Coast Main Line passenger trains have occurred – not exclusively at weekends – and of course there has been the plethora of regular steam excursions taking advantage of the fine scenery in all seasons.

Closure by BR was strongly possible in the 1980s but fortunately public protest and increased passenger use meant that such was not carried out, and a more secure future assured. In January 2017, after a large landslip at Eden Brows (north of Armathwaite) caused the southbound line to be closed between Howe & Co's sidings and Culgaith, a radical and innovative design for rebuilding the embankment was adopted by Network Rail, which classified the project as the most difficult repair job it had ever undertaken. Such a vote of confidence helps the line to continue to provide the valuable service evident today, a genuine tribute to the tough, hard-working navvies that gave so much at its time of construction.

Newcastle Bridges: King Edward Bridge, Metro Bridge, High Level Bridge, Swing Bridge, The Tyne Bridge, 15 August 2009.

An impressive and spectacular array of bridges that cross the River Tyne, each in its own fashion, stitches together the different components of this scene as if with the careful crafting of an expert jigsaw creator. Each bridge facilitates the necessary traversal of the Tyne in different modes.

Taking each mode as we move downriver, the nearest is King Edward Bridge which carries East Coast Main Line trains, then the blue Metro Bridge which conveys light-rail trains linking each side of the river, built for the Tyne and Wear Passenger Transport Executive. High Level Bridge is the oldest of the existing bridges, designed by the famed railway engineer Robert Stephenson, jointly with Thomas Elliot Harrison, with two decks. The upper deck is for the railway and the lower for the road, which is now used only for buses and taxis. The red Swing Bridge was important for allowing improved shipment of coal but now opens mainly for pleasure boats. The arched Tyne Bridge has become the icon of the Tyne, and reminds us about Tyneside's industrial past and promising regeneration. The great arch span is 531 feet long and rises to a height of 170 feet. Finally we can just glimpse the Gateshead Millennium Bridge which is the River Tyne's only foot and cycle bridge, and as a tilting bridge it is a world-first. Its six spans, four of which are directly over the river, allow a clear headway of 83 ft at High Water.

Royal Border Bridge: EWS Class 66 66158 heads towards Berwick-upon-Tweed station with HTA coal hoppers bound for Millerhill, early evening, 18 April 2003.

This long and grandiose twenty-eight arch curved viaduct doesn't quite cross the true border between England and Scotland – which is a little to the north of Berwick – but it always looks fine when reflected in the waters of the River Tweed, whether viewed on its eastern facade in morning light or, as here, in the setting sun on the western flank. In steam days, photographers were helped in capturing on film the viaduct's impressive length when the trail of silhouetted steam from the locomotive highlighted its progress to the north or south accompanied by the march of the arches below it. Less easy with a diesel, although the maroon and yellow livery of the locomotive means it still features as a worthy part of the scene. The arches of the road bridges mirror those of the railway viaduct as we look east. It was Queen Victoria who opened the bridge in 1850, bestowing it with the rare honour of incorporating the word 'Royal' into the bridge's name. We proudly celebrate and conserve such majestic monuments, but Robert Stephenson, who as engineer deployed his technical skills in designing and building this bridge, actually constructed it at its northern end straight through the ramparts of the then 500-year-old Berwick Castle, thus demolishing most of its remains in the process. It is claimed that some of the stones were reused in the bridge itself.

Above: Royal Border Bridge: A Class 801 'Azuma' passes with an East Coast Main Line service, late afternoon, 4 September 2020.

While similar to the Great Western new breed of high speed electric units, these London North Eastern Railway units have a greater level of seating comfort and in many a shared viewpoint a snazzy livery which, kept clean, looks more interesting than the darker green provided for the Great Western fleet. They have certainly helped transform the speed and frequency of the service between London King's Cross and Edinburgh, and the Class 800 bi-mode units also carry a relatively powerful diesel engine too. This has helped on such occasions as the author encountered when his train was cancelled at Stevenage owing to overhead wires damaged on the Peterborough route, and the alternative service was diverted via Cambridge, Ely and March – all non-electrified territory. In fact it was quite an experience to cross timeless Fenland lanes traversing level crossings in a state-of-the-art new train.

Opposite: Kinghorn Viaduct: A Class 800 bi-mode 'Azuma' passes with the 12.00 London King's Cross to Inverness, 11 September 2020.

Demonstrating the versatility of the new 'Azuma' Class 800 bi-mode units on an eight-hour journey from London to and through the Highlands, we see this train on an otherwise non-electrified commuter route passing alongside the Fife coast with the Firth of Forth and the coastline immediately east of Edinburgh in the background. It's a scenic route and passengers will also enjoy passing several distilleries and plenty of Highland sheep and cattle on their way to Inverness. While in Scotland it will inevitably pass one type of train it has displaced – the Class 43 HSTs, admittedly from the fleet sent north from Great Western territory. Their appearance with ScotRail in shortened versions on the 'Inter7City' routes replacing Class 170 diesel multiple units has in its own way also radicalised the quality of ride for the many tourists and travellers using the train to reach their undoubtedly scenic locations.

Opposite: Loch Awe: A ScotRail Class 156 amidst autumnal colours with a mid-afternoon service from Oban to Glasgow, 20 October 2019.

This station is popular with commuters, both schoolchildren and business folk, and it serves an attractive original railway hotel located immediately above it with a direct set of stairs that climb steeply from the up platform. The down train drivers have especially good reasons to keep alert, as within a mile or so there are tripwires below steep cutting walls where rock fall poses a threat to line security. Here however, while paused, they can observe the loch in all its Highland beauty and scenic splendour. You can even stay by the line here in one of the last remaining Scottish camping coaches available for private hire. Don't be too concerned by the close proximity of the early morning passing service which might just waken you – you'll be able to pop down to the lakeside to catch a fish for breakfast!

Below: Loch Awe Side Viaduct: A ScotRail Class 156 operates a morning service to Oban just after sunrise, 31 October 2019.

The mid-autumnal sunrise on a crisp, tranquil Scottish morning is just in time to allow for this local service train to partake in the loch's absolute calm and peace as it crosses the viaduct here over the River Orchy. All is surrounded by the mantle of golden colours magnificently worn by the brackens and foliage on the Highland mountains which dominate, seemingly watching as sentries over the transforming scene as daylight returns after the cool chill of the night. Boundaries of language can only hint at the awesome and unrivalled atmosphere of this truly Scottish splendour.

Loch Awe camping coach: Sunset view of loch and railway carriage, 2 November 2019.

An interesting aspect of the modern railway is the continuing tradition of camping coaches found in several locations in the UK, including a significant number at Dawlish Warren. They originally provided economic accommodation for railway employees' families in which to take their holidays and were very popular because of the scenic locations in which they were provided. Some were even ex-Pullman carriages, such as that found at Corfe Castle and Lyndhurst Road. It was a condition of the holiday that travel to and from these camping coaches was by train. Intriguingly, for those staying at camping coaches located at stations on the Alnwick to Coldstream North Eastern Railway (NER) branch line, their travel along the branch after its closure to passengers was by a carriage specially attached to the daily parcels train. The coach featured here is especially blessed by a spectacular sunset, unusually during a fine, dry spell of weather in mid-autumn. Sunsets are always difficult to capture at their best because of the gradually descending sun which sometimes provides its best kaleidoscope of colours both when setting and after it has set. The author has several local favourite sunset locations overlooking Mount Edgcumbe and the Tamar estuary in south-west Devon and he usually can't decide which are his best sunset colours as the same sunset changes from red through to bright orange and thence to crimson before fading to salmon pink.

This camping coach is situated very close to Loch Awe station and also to the splendid Loch Awe Hotel which dominates this scene off camera. Residents staying in the coach even have their own garden! Such a superb viewpoint must surely be among the most naturally scenic of landscapes in Britain that can be viewed both from a passing train and from a static carriage.

Chapter 2
THE NARROW GAUGE RAILWAY LANDSCAPE

Cornwall, Dobwalls Miniature Railway: Rio Grande 2-8-2 498 *Otto Mears*, 1 July 2006. Locomotives are approximately 1/8th scale; gauge is 7ft ¼in (184mm).

   The water tank, wooden trestle bridge and locomotive driver's uniform each contribute to this atmospheric recreation of the US rail scene, alongside the authentic detail on the locomotive itself. This is based on a Baldwin Class K-37 Mikado built in 1902 as operated by the Denver and Rio Grande Western (D&RGW). The full-size original locomotive was rebuilt in 1930 into a narrow gauge outside frame Mikado by the D&RGW at its Burnham shops in Denver, keeping the original boiler and cab, and using new cylinders, a new frame and a narrow gauge wheel set . Such immense detail in this scale model is extraordinary; it requires no stretch of the imagination to conjure up an authentic image of the original. Unfortunately, for a variety of reasons, the Dobwalls complex is no longer in existence but all memories associated with its heyday are full of admiration and respect from the many enthusiasts who visited it.

Above: Cornwall, Dobwalls Miniature Railway: US Union Pacific 4-8-8-4 'Big Boy' X4008 *William Jeffers*, 1 July 2006. Scale is the same as *Otto Mears*.

John Southern's famed miniature railway was based on two American railroad routes and I was lucky enough to pay a visit as John's guest before the season started, while making arrangements for a visit from the Plymouth Railway Circle. I had not previously visited the site and was astonished by the complex and meticulous detail given to each of the locomotives in the collection. This small scale giant looks like it will be a very snug fit for its full length to be accommodated on that turntable! The 'Big Boys', twenty-five of which were built from 1941 to 1944 by the American Locomotive Company, were in service with the Union Pacific Railroad until 1959, mainly hauling freight. Their weight of 560 tons and power of 6,920hp underlined the fact that these were the largest and heaviest steam locomotives ever built. The diesel-electric locomotives that replaced them may well have been easier and cheaper to maintain, but were certainly less impressive than these noisy, smoke-belching mammoths of steam, each with its harmony of many moving parts. In May 2019 'Big Boy' 4014 was returned to service in a journey across the Midwest to mark the 150th anniversary of the completion of the Transcontinental Railroad in 1869.

Opposite: New Mills, Launceston Steam Railway: 2ft gauge Darjeeling Himalayan Railway, India 0-4-0STWT+T locomotive No. 19 runs around the 12.00 ex-Launceston, 1 September 2009.

On my 'bucket list' is a journey on the Darjeeling Himalayan Railway! Until such time, this impressive Indian visitor to the Launceston Steam Railway more than suffices. It is seen appropriately decorated with a garland, for these floral tributes are usually provided for statues of the Hindu gods and goddesses in the temples where they reside or when carried in procession. It isn't too much to stretch the imagination and suggest that an offering of worship with this garland is due in response to the awe and wonder bestowed by this blue goddess. Built in 1889 by Sharp, Stewart & Co. at their Glasgow Atlas works, the very graceful interaction of the gliding connecting rods and steam cylinders is both fascinating and intriguing to watch and hear.

Above: Colyford, Seaton Tramway: Tram 11 crosses the A3052 operating an early afternoon service from Seaton to Colyton, 12 September 2009.

Trams pass alongside the River Axe estuary before needing to cross the A3052 along which traffic hurtles between the two sides of the valley, and the paused cars and caravan draw the attention of those on board towards this tram with its attractive livery of beige and cream. The level crossing is open-gated and relies on motorists safely obeying the red flashing lights. The tram driver proceeds ahead at caution after sounding warning hoots. Fortunately, no one is taking the inevitable risk of attempting to cross once the lights are activated but before the tram has actually passed over.

Opposite above: Colyford, Seaton Tramway: Tram 9 arrives at Colyford station en route from Colyton to Seaton, 12 September 2009. This is a hybrid design based on the old Plymouth and Blackburn trams.

This three-mile narrow gauge tramway is built partly on the route of the LSWR branch to Seaton from Axminster, closed 7 March 1966. The exquisite fleet of trams offers a vista from their open-top balconies over the beautiful marshland and reed beds alongside the River Axe, home to an abundance of wildlife and with a special attraction for bird watchers. Best of course to take a ride on a late summer's day, as here, when the sun is still strong enough to cheer the evident throngs of visitors still taking a holiday in sunny Devon.

Opposite below: Black Hole Marsh (Axe Valley), Seaton Tramway: Tram 16 approaches Colyford station, while passing with a driver-training unscheduled service heading for Colyton, 12 September 2009.

The origins of this immaculate vintage tram, Bournemouth Corporation Tramways open top car 106 (3ft. 6in gauge), date back to 1921. It was withdrawn on the closure of the Bournemouth system in 1936, rebuilt at Seaton between 1974 and 1991 and reintroduced to service in 1992. The learner driver may well have his mind on the route, but he could be forgiven for glancing over his shoulder at that attractive East Devon scenery through which this line passes. 'Black Hole Marsh' in the Axe Valley was the original name given to this part of the estuary, now a new wetland for the Seaton wetlands reserve and forming a large saltwater lagoon after having been a freshwater marsh for the past 150 years.

Bressingham Garden Railway: 10¼in gauge 0-4-0 ST No. 1 *Alan Bloom*, modelled on the Hunslet Engine Co. quarry design, 27 October 2007.

Set in the picturesque gardens and parkland of Bressingham, here is a fine ride through the autumnal boughs and leaves of the birch and oak trees that abound along the routes of the various railways (of differing gauges) found at this unique location. There is much to entertain the steam railway enthusiasts and families out for adventure in the encompassing woodlands and countryside. It's somewhere you can spend your whole day travelling around the site or simply taking a gentle stroll among the flowerbeds and landscape gardens. Every now and then, you'll stumble across one of the miniature or narrow gauge railways as they cross your path. A real feast for everyone!

Bressingham Garden Railway: No. 1 *Alan Bloom*, 27 October 2007.

Bressingham's tribute to autumn with its rich reds, yellows and golds embellishing its carefully nurtured gardens and hedges matches the fine maroon and red of the locomotive, which seems cheerfully at home hauling its load of contented passengers around this rich arboretum. Although somewhat dwarfed by the surrounding shrubbery, the steam and smoke accompanied by the quiet whistle all remind us that this little locomotive holds an important place in the hearts and minds across the generations – for it enthuses the young children aboard who will perhaps become steam engine drivers themselves as a result of their admiration of their wise, if aged, driver.

Carrog, Llangollen Railway: Hunslet 0-4-0ST locomotive 823 *Irish Mail* in shunting demonstrations, 18 April 2009. Gauge is 2ft.

Somewhat dwarfed by GWR 4500 Class 2-6-2T 5526 on the left, this attractive saddle tank locomotive is certainly the older statesman, having been built in 1903. It served at Dinorwic Slate Quarry, Llanberis, until November 1969 and now rests at its usual home of the West Lancashire Light Railway, where it no longer needs to contemplate steep inclines and mountainous territory. It is built with a cab – which is unusual for a quarry locomotive – and fully benefits from the crimson red and gold outlines bestowed by its livery. The comparison in size between the two veterans says much about the territory that such quarry locomotives worked, requiring agility to tackle sharp curves and ascents beyond the remit of that achieved by standard gauge locomotives.

Aberglaslyn Pass, Welsh Highland Railway: 7863 2-6-2 + 2-6-2T NGG16, No. 138, ex-South African Railways, one of the last Garratts built by Beyer-Peacock, hauling the 12.10 Caernarfon to Beddgelert and Pont Croesor, 30 May 2010.

The Aberglaslyn Pass is a spectacular river-cut steep-sided valley where the water can rise to the level of the railway bridge after torrential rain over the Snowdon range. Here the water is calm, the spring rains having subsided, and shows no turbulence to concern those travelling in the passing train. The installation of the bridge was essential in order for the railway to extend towards its intended destination of Porthmadog. No. 138 is oil fired here, but later was converted to coal firing during 2012, and its steaming on coal for the first time was during early October 2012. Unlike many narrow gauge steam locomotives, there is plenty of room for the crew to stand up inside the cab. It certainly provides adequate shelter from the frequent showers and rain that this part of Wales often enjoys.

Opposite above: Aberglaslyn Pass, Welsh Highland Railway: 7863, 30 May 2010.

The towering sides and rocky crags of the valley attempt to envelop the sleek train, drifting across the tapestry with its matching reds only broken by the authentic umber and cream applied to the Pullman carriage immediately behind the locomotive. Yet the very size of the locomotive and the long rake of carriages means it exudes its own presence, with the sound of the passing train infusing the valley with the echo of past times when much smaller narrow gauge locomotives hauling mineral and passenger trains first traversed the route.

Opposite below: As the train breaks free from the enshrouding valley, and is met by a splash of purple colour to welcome its escape, so the brooding hills of the Snowdon range start to beckon. They portend a stiff climb ahead and there will be much to keep the locomotive crew busy as the line twists and turns around the contours of the Welsh hills. Passengers in the Pullman car are well placed to enjoy the sound of the locomotive's distinctive motion.

Below: Near Rhyd Ddu, Welsh Highland Railway: 7863 2-6-2 + 2-6-2T NGG16, No. 138, seen hauling the 14.45 Pont Croesor to Beddgelert and Caernarfon, 30 May 2010.

Leaning into the curve we find this impressive locomotive working ever harder as it climbs closer to the Snowdon range with, in the background, Moel Eilio, at 726m (2,382ft) asserting its presence. The astounding scenery on this line is equal to any of that in Scotland and fully justifies the use of the word 'Highland' to describe the nominal route of the line. These giants of the narrow gauge certainly aren't overwhelmed by such terrain and the red livery proves an eye catching embellishment to the unfolding majestic vista.

Near Waunfawr, Welsh Highland Railway: 7863 2-6-2 + 2-6-2T NGG16, No. 138 seen hauling the 14.45 Pont Croesor to Beddgelert and Caernarfon, 30 May 2010.

The distant mountain acknowledges with a salute the very size of these Garratt locomotives, for each inspires awe and conveys an impression of the strength and solidity that they individually possess. Maybe the mythical Welsh dragon draws its breath from within the framework of the locomotive? Is that steam or dragon's breath that escapes into the cooler air of the Welsh mountains? Here the train bustles along having conquered the demands of the climb and the final section of descent to Caernarfon is now well underway. Caernarfon station now has a fine modern terminus building which was completed in March 2019, and houses on permanent display a 3ft gauge 1893-built ex-Penmaenmawr granite quarry 0-4-0 De Winton locomotive.

Near Rhyd Ddu, Welsh Highland Railway: 3267 2-6-2 + 2-6-2T NGG16, No. 87, hauling the 14.40 Caernarfon to Beddgelert and Pont Croesor, 30 May 2010.

This coal-fired locomotive entered service in early 2009. Its addition made sure there was an adequate fleet in place ready for the opening of the complete Welsh Highland Railway in the same year, giving three working NGG16s to form the core fleet. The newly applied midnight blue livery looks very smart, and through the open windows the passengers relish the sound of this hard-working machine as it commences the steep descent to Beddgelert.

Opposite: Near Betws Garmon, Welsh Highland Railway: 3267 2-6-2 + 2-6-2T NGG16, No. 87, ex-South African Railways, seen hauling the 10.00 Caernarfon to Pont Croesor, 31 May 2010.

It is as if, daunted by the claw-like steeply-sided mountain sweeping down to the valley, the train is making its escape, highlighted by the rays of sunlight which provide relief and contrast to the darker shadows of the raw nature from which it flees. The stark folds in the rock allow little soil for trees to establish enough depth for their roots, and the barren surfaces reinforce the dominance of this rocky giant. It can be compared to Goliath's awesome strength when overshadowing David's small physique, even though size, as we know from that story, isn't everything and the train has the victory as it emerges, undefeated, into the sunlit verdant meadow. Quite what our bovine friend makes of it all we can only guess – certainly the train is being given an unflinching stare. Will this become a further encounter between challengers each restraining their quietly implicit hidden strength?

Below: Afon Hwch, Lower Viaduct, Snowdon Mountain Railway: 2838 0-4-2T rack locomotive No. 6 *Padarn* with the 12.00 departure from Llanberis station, 31 May 2010. Gauge is 2ft 7½in.

With an average gradient of 1 in 7.86, and at its steepest 1 in 5.5, it is understandable that the Swiss Locomotive and Machine Works of Winterthur acquired the contract to build the Snowdon Mountain Railway's locomotives. This was because at the time the railway was being planned, only the Swiss had significant experience in building rack locomotives. The engine meanwhile here steadily pushes its single carriage away from the terminus at the foot of the mountain as the teeth of the rack engage with the locomotive's pinion teeth for the grand ascent. It's a fine day and the fortunate passengers can look forward to a magnificent panorama from the top.

Above: Hebron, Snowdon Mountain Railway: 0-4-2T rack locomotive No. 3 *Wyddfa* descends with the late morning train from Summit to Llanberis station, 31 May 2010.

Somewhat dwarfed by the lower reaches of Snowdon, amidst clouds scurrying by as they pass over pastel shades of spring greens shared by random clumps of trees, rocks and sheep pastures, the locomotive eases from its strenuous efforts as it approaches the penultimate station on its descent. At 326m it is still 218m above Llanberis station, but the grade is gentler and the warm sunshine disguises the head of steam still available to the driver.

Opposite: Near Halfway station (500m), Snowdon Mountain Railway: 0-4-2T rack locomotive No. 3 *Wyddfa* ascends with a mid-afternoon train from Llanberis station to Summit, 31 May 2010.

Those tempted by fine weather to walk up Snowdon by following the footpath that dovetails the railway will find that the gradient is not too steep and sometimes these folk are to be seen wearing sandals and just t-shirts for their journey. However, it is unlikely they will have anticipated the bleak and sparse slopes of the higher parts of the mountain where the cooler air and potentially volatile weather conditions can suddenly pose a challenge to such explorers. Best always to check the safety advice for taking sensible clothing and equipment.

The ascending train passes, in the background, the soaring heights of Moel Cynghorian's 674m (2,211ft). Its southern slopes are gentle, while the northern aspect is precipitous. Driver and fireman have been working steadily to coax their steed forwards as it clambers up the severe gradient. The boilers of these steam locomotives are inclined at an angle of 9°, to keep the water level over the tubes when the locomotive is ascending the mountain – the locomotive necessarily always runs chimney-first up the mountain. The rack at Snowdon utilises a pair of toothed racks which can be seen ahead of the train as it threads its way up to the passing loop.

Near Halfway Station (500m), Snowdon Mountain Railway: 2838 0-4-2T rack locomotive No. 6 *Padarn* descends with the 13.30 departure from Summit to Llanberis station, 31 May 2010.

While not offering an equal match for such Swiss alpine routes as the Rigi Bahnen on which regular steam operates, the Snowdon Mountain Railway proves a veritable contender, for the Welsh mountains hold sway with their presence and rigour, and its locomotives all share much in the way of character and technical initiative. In fact, in August 2018 one of the locomotives from the Brienz Rothorn Bahn (BRB) mountain railway in Switzerland was brought over to join its sister locomotives operating on Snowdon. The BRB and Snowdon Mountain Railway use the same rack and pinion rail system and their steam engines were built in the same Swiss factory over 125 years ago. While the BRB ascends to the 2,350m summit of Brienzer Rothorn, the highest in the Emmental Alps, in comparison Snowdon stands over 1,200m shorter than its Swiss counterpart. It is clear that everyone in this full carriage certainly considers the breathtaking journey to and from the summit of Snowdon worth every minute.

Birkenhead Woodside, Birkenhead Wirral Heritage Tramway: Tram 70 passes the old dock gates (built 1868) at the entrance to Shore Road, 15 April 2009.

Appearing somewhat out of place, at least in Birkenhead, is Tram 70 which is one of two Hong Kong tramcars built new in 1992 as a special purchase by the Wirral Transport Museum and shipped to Birkenhead courtesy of P&O Ferries. It is appropriately finished in the colours of the old Birkenhead Corporation and trundles along a short line between Birkenhead Woodside and the museum. The setting is certainly one of northern suburbia, clearly given a clean-up and looking attractive in its red brick, which all helps to integrate the maroon and cream hue that authentically recalls that which adorned Birkenhead's very first trams. In Hong Kong, similar trams run on a dedicated tramway and must contend with crowds, heat and humidity, neon lights and even, increasingly, demonstrations and protests.

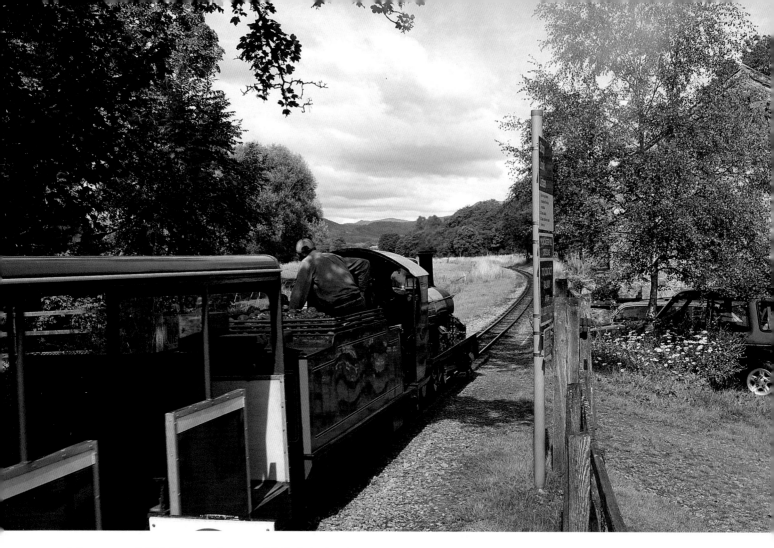

Muncaster Mill, Ravenglass and Eskdale Railway: 15in gauge 0-8-2 *River Irt* awaits departure with the 15.20 from Ravenglass to Dalegarth, 13 August 2009.

The driver peers ahead, no doubt contemplating the terrain through which this train will pass on its spectacular journey on 'La'al Ratty' through this remote part of Lakeland. There's a good load of coal in the tender, ensuring that the destination is achieved successfully. The green livery of the locomotive blends very well with the summer greens of the grasses and the leaves of the trees. *River Irt* is the oldest working 15in gauge locomotive in the world, built in 1894. Here she looks in fine fettle with a very clean head of steam and a brisk readiness to tackle the gradients which lie ahead, some as steep as 1 in 55. Such a lifetime of memories must provide plenty to keep her reminiscing as she faithfully continues to fulfil her current purpose of carrying travellers into the heart of the Lake District.

Chapter 3

THE PRESERVED DIESELS LANDSCAPE

Bodmin Parkway, Bodmin and Wenford Railway: Class 50 50042 *Triumph* in 1970s BR blue livery, preserved at the Bodmin Steam Railway, arrives with the 14.00 from Bodmin, 29 March 2009.

The shadows cast by the springtime trees awaiting their time to blossom wave their branches gently over this branch line invader as it descends to Bodmin Parkway station. 'Invader' is certainly appropriate because this fleet of fifty locomotives was named after Royal Navy warships or shore establishments. They were always very popular with enthusiasts because of their distinctive 'roar', emitted when they accelerated (for which they received the nickname 'Hoovers'). These locomotives drew criticism from BR Southern Region for the pounding they supposedly gave the tracks of the LSWR route from London to Exeter via Salisbury when they were allocated to passenger duties on that route. The author recalls their equally halcyon days when they were first introduced to the Crewe to Preston and Scotland route, on which they double-headed many express passenger trains. BR London Midland Region seemed to have no such reservations about their performance.

Bodmin Parkway, Bodmin and Wenford Railway: Class 37 37142 in 1970s BR blue livery, preserved at the Bodmin and Wenford Railway, 29 March 2009.

Evidence of sleeper replacement amidst rusting rails and a rather neglected gradient post at least suggests that the Bodmin and Wenford Railway permanent way team will be along some time to install the new wooden sleepers – a thankless task, no doubt. It's a reminder of the sort of work carried out by volunteers at the many preserved railways around the country. Some people are involved with maintenance of the permanent way, rolling stock and station buildings, while other roles include selling merchandise and tickets, acting as station staff or looking after a museum. Some will fulfil the role of guard, involved in the safe despatch and journey of the train and its passengers, others will have the high profile tasks of driving the locomotives or signalling. Then there's the gardening and grounds – all of these roles invite volunteers who receive the requisite training to exercise their chosen area of potential expertise. Why not get involved in your local heritage railway if you have yet to try it? The rewards of comradeship and achievement are assured.

Buckfastleigh, South Devon Railway: Class 20 20096 in BR Blue livery, owned by Harry Needle, with evening milk tanks en route to Bishops Bridge, 12 June 2005.

The attraction provided by the heritage railway sector is that you can put together all sorts of fictional operations that *might* have happened, with a splash of historicity contained within certain aspects of such – just not all at the same time or location! This means that the railway in the landscape of the preserved railway may not be authentic in all that is revealed. Yet no one is complaining about this feature here with a Class 20 working in the West Country, when they were essentially a BR Scottish or Eastern Region locomotive, hauling a most unlikely load of milk tanks. This does not matter – the trip freight that Class 20s mainly worked would have seen a great variety of wagons, rather than milk, that needed to get to the distributors by next morning. You can guess which British Railways Region is recalled by the white Scotty dog emblem.

Opposite: Buckfastleigh, South Devon Railway: 'Deltic' Class 55 55019 *Royal Highland Fusilier* in BR blue livery arrives with a late afternoon service from Totnes, 12 June 2005.

Very much a visitor to these parts of the UK, the roar of the Napier Deltic engines never fails to impress and here ensures a dramatic arrival by 55019 *Royal Highland Fusilier* at Buckfastleigh – rather different from its usual termini of London King's Cross or Edinburgh while in service with BR. The blue livery actually suited these locomotives very well and the red name plates helped to add differentiation. The presentation of the locomotive is immaculate and a credit to the preservation of such a magnificent machine.

Below: Buckfastleigh, South Devon Railway: *Royal Highland Fusilier* arrives with an empty coaching stock positioning movement, 12 June 2005.

The lush green of the rolling Devonshire hills and the palm trees here providing a reminder of Devon's warmer climate as they greet this welcome visitor as it encounters the various trappings of a preservation station. Here we see such traditional ingredients as semaphore signals, a footbridge and water tower all helping to accommodate an engrossing atmosphere. The platform is not in public use, but a colourful horticultural display can be admired by the passengers opposite as they await their steam train's arrival.

Above: Caddaford Curve, South Devon Railway: Class 04 D2246 with the 12.00 from Buckfastleigh to Totnes, 4 November 2006.

The River Dart, which this train will follow for the length of its journey, makes its way towards Totnes and Dartmouth. It's a tranquil location for this shunter with its chevrons ('wasp stripes') that create the distinctive black and yellow warning which gave such locomotives added visibility while working in the railway yards and sidings of their usual terrain. Such was all part of the railway scene in the latter days of steam, and provides here a contrast to the blue sky and amber autumnal colour of the leaves.

Opposite above: Hood Bridge, South Devon Railway: Class 33 33002, in Civil Engineers 'Dutch' livery, hauls a demonstration freight for Plymouth Railway Circle, 22 June 2009.

The evening glow highlights the cab of this Class 33, a traditional Southern Region locomotive in BR days. Within the borders of Devon these engines did see service on trains along the 'Southern' line from London Waterloo to Exeter and on services from Exeter to Barnstaple and Paignton; they were also occasional visitors to Okehampton in connection with heavy stone ballast trains from Meldon Quarry. Their relative light weight would have suited such duties as a typical engineers train recreated here. The familiar chug of their Sulzer engines made them popular with enthusiasts, especially when they appeared along Weymouth tramway or, occasionally in pairs on the East Devon banks when in charge of London trains.

Opposite below: River Dart, South Devon Railway: Class 31 31101 approaches Hood Bridge with the 17.15 train from Buckfastleigh, passing by the tranquil waters of the River Dart, 21 July 2019.

The low water level in the River Dart permits a reflection not available when the river is in full flow after overnight rains. In fact the photographer would not be standing on the rock where he is under such circumstances! This locomotive normally resides at the Avon Valley Railway and spent much of its early working life based at Stratford depot. It had the privilege of hauling the Royal Train with Her Majesty the Queen on board for a visit to Tattenham Corner station for the Epsom Derby race day meeting on 4 July 1969. The GWR chocolate and cream colours carried by the auto coach contrast relatively comfortably with the carmine and cream carried by most of the remaining carriages. It is at this location that the first train of the day to Totnes usually disturbs an owl and occasionally a kingfisher, as both have been seen by the author while on board when observing the approach of the train to Hood Bridge in his capacity as train guard.

Approaching Hood Bridge, South Devon Railway: Class 37/3 D6737 (37037/37321) *Loch Treig* hauls the 12.40 from Buckfastleigh to Totnes, 4 November 2006.

Autumnal red hues embrace the river bank and leaves of the surrounding trees, accompanied by the golden brown of the rails and sleepers, as the countryside bathes in the warmth of mid-autumn early afternoon sunshine. This tranquil calm is briefly disturbed by the growl of the locomotive as it plays hide and seek with the shadows while in no hurry to convey its train to the next station. It is quite likely that it will be looped at Bishops Bridge to await the passing of the down train before entering Staverton station.

Hood Bridge, South Devon Railway: Class 37/3 37314 visiting from the Midland Railway with an afternoon service from Totnes to Buckfastleigh, 10 June 2006.

Some Class 37s in Scotland wore BR Large Logo livery, as seen here: blue with yellow cabs, grey roof, large numbers and full bodyside height BR logos. It made a change from the more regular standard BR blue and has proved popular in preservation. Given the length of the locomotive and carriages, it will be quite a tight fit at Buckfastleigh's platform. Such should be no problem in view of the fact that the South Devon Railway has played host to Class 37 locomotives over a number of years. Their characteristic growl was frequently heard on the china clay trains that would have been seen on the main line at Totnes where it bypasses the preserved line. This example of the class is certainly presented in immaculate paintwork which reflects nicely in the river and the exhaust emissions indicates a steady roar as the locomotive accelerates away towards Buckfastleigh.

Opposite: Hood Bridge, South Devon Railway: Class 33 D6501 alongside the low water level of the River Dart in the summer heat of 2018, as it approaches Hood Bridge, replacing the usual steam locomotive, 15 July.

It is unusual to see the River Dart this low –such a contrast with the springtime flow of water after heavy rain when the water level can be very much closer to the rails. Dartmoor becomes tinder dry in these conditions and the babble of stream water flowing into rivers such as the Dart slows to a dribble. During very dry summers, it is not uncommon on heritage steam lines for steam locomotives to be replaced by diesels in order to avoid lineside fires which can be very easily caused by a rogue spark from the chimney – and resulting fires can cause a lot of problems to signalling. The hot summer weather is not best for business on such a line as this, for the lure of the nearby beaches is often viewed by the general public as more inviting than going inland for a riverside rail trip. Even so, the presence of the river helps cool down the surroundings – and train crew.

Below: Staverton, South Devon Railway: Class 37/3 37321 and 37314 (the latter a guest from the Midland Railway) arrive with a late afternoon service from Totnes to Buckfastleigh, 10 June 2006.

These Class 37 locomotives are very popular both in preservation and on the national rail network. They still find occasional employment on passenger trains, such as working with substitute stock provided where there is a shortage of available diesel multiple units such as in East Anglia, Cumbria and South Wales. Here the surrounding valley will reverberate with their characteristic English Electric growl once they depart from the station. The crossing box, gates and semaphore signals along with the colourful metallic advertising signs remind us of the various elements which combine to create the atmosphere of the steam age, yet as this class of locomotive worked alongside steam in parts of the Eastern Region, we can allow such an anachronism. It seems as if they are edging around these features, careful to respect the railway landscape in which they take part.

Staverton, South Devon Railway: Class 37/3 37321 and 37314 depart with a late afternoon service from Totnes to Buckfastleigh, 10 June 2006.

Here we see the same Class 37s featured in the previous photograph passing by a Ruston and Hornsby 0-4-0 diesel hydraulic shunter which, in its active service in industry, provided shunting duties at the Central Electricity Generating Board (CEGB) power station at Staythorpe, Newark, and at British Gypsum, Newark. The cramped space for the sidings is typical of preserved railways where available space is often taken up with the many and varied items of rolling stock which they have acquired over time. Both vehicles here are in commendable external condition and convey a sense of the care and attention provided by the large volunteer groups responsible for their upkeep. That sense of belonging to a 'family' with shared interests and of feeling valued in such roles is a very important part of the reason why preserved railways, both small and large, have flourished as they have become established over time. Such friendships provide confidence and self-respect based on trust, so fulfilling an irreplaceable part of life in an otherwise potentially lonely world.

Washford Bank, West Somerset Railway: 'Warship' Class 42 D821 *Greyhound,* preserved at the Severn Valley Railway, hauls the 14.00 Bishops Lydeard to Minehead, 12 June 2010.

Looking a marvellous sight and emitting a splendid hydraulic 'hum' as it ascends Washford Bank, this powerful locomotive is well-suited to its maroon livery with the small yellow front panels. The majority of the 'Warship' Class wore BR green and only fourteen were honoured to carry these distinguished colours. They echo the determination by BR Western Region to continue the tradition of the GWR in applying distinctive colours that kept their trains 'different' from 'the others'. D821 is a 1960 Swindon-built engine and therefore a Western Region thoroughbred, even though it migrated to the Southern Region later in its relatively short life. All of the class had been withdrawn by 1972. It is easy to see why they attracted the sort of following which had also accompanied many steam classes, and why essentially 'steam-only' photographers permitted themselves to photograph these impressive stars.

Washford Bank, West Somerset Railway: front locomotive 'Hymek' Class 35 D7017 leads with GWR 5101 Class 2-6-2T 4160 behind, both preserved at the West Somerset Railway, 12 June 2010.

Evoking memories from an era when an occasional pairing of two contrasting types of motive power occurred, often owing to problems with the diesel rather than the steam locomotive, we see two proud locomotives, both with immaculate paintwork, as they clamber up Washford Bank. The Western Region engineers who considered the BR 1955 modernisation plan realised that, unlike their counterparts on the West and East Coast routes, electrification would not reach their territory and so they sought alternative forms of diesel power. Hydraulic transmission had proved successful in its use on the Continent and it was seen as offering potential; hence its adoption by BR Western Region.

The two-tone green of the Hymek is especially appealing, along with the BR lion and wheel emblem on the side. The different greens of the two locomotives' liveries are certainly complimentary to each other as they accommodate the rampant summer foliage also unfurling its wings.

Near Williton, West Somerset Railway: Class 47 D1661 *North Star*, preserved at the West Somerset Railway, hauls the 15.40 Minehead to Bishops Lydeard past Egrove Farm near Williton, 14 June 2008.

 The two-tone green of the BR Class 47s certainly looks smart as applied to this example, with the greens of the crops providing a supportive role. The reddish hue of the West Somerset soils helps the locomotive to stand out, a colour shared by the bricks used in the local farmhouses. The rolling countryside starts to give way to the higher ground of the Quantocks rising in the background. The day's heat has produced some clouds giving just a risk of a shower – which will no doubt be welcomed for the dry soil by the hard-working farmers.

Above: Castle Hill, West Somerset Railway: 'Western' Class 52 D1062 *Western Courier*, preserved at the Severn Valley Railway, hauls a mid-afternoon train from Bishops Lydeard to Minehead, 12 June 2010.

Shining in immaculate maroon paintwork, this 'Western' has enjoyed a gradual roll down the gradients from Bishops Lydeard and will soon face the climb up Washford Bank. With two Maybach engines providing 2,700hp, that shouldn't pose any problems for the locomotive crew. The attractive scenery of the Quantocks will soon be replaced by views across the Bristol Channel towards South Wales. Interestingly, the Westerns worked frequently to Cardiff and Swansea, and yet the distance between these cities and this part of Somerset travelling by land is vast when compared to that directly as the crow flies.

Opposite above: Castle Hill, West Somerset Railway: 'Warship' Class 42 D821 *Greyhound*, preserved at the Severn Valley Railway, hauls the 16.00 Minehead to Bishops Lydeard, 12 June 2010.

All of the 'Warships' began their working lives almost exclusively on passenger trains as their low weight for braking hindered their use on loose-coupled freight trains. In fact they were to be found mainly on the Paddington to Bristol and Paddington to Penzance routes in their early years. Such terrain as evident here, with the start of the ascent alongside the edge of the Quantocks, would have been encountered by these locomotives on the Devon and Cornwall banks and *Greyhound* appears more than content with its trailing load as it enjoys responding to the challenge of the climb ahead.

Opposite below: Near Bicknoller, West Somerset Railway: Class 47 D1661 *North Star*, preserved at the West Somerset Railway, hauling the 17.25 Bishops Lydeard to Minehead, 14 June 2008.

As in my comment accompanying the photograph of this locomotive being passed by West Country Pacific 34046 *Braunton* at Williton (see p. 168), BR green livery certainly complemented some of the classes to which it was applied, and in particular there is no dispute about its splendid adornment of Class 47s. The pastoral scene demonstrates the typical English summer countryside at its picturesque best, and with the sound of the train resounding off the rolling hills as it threads its way through this rural tapestry. The viewer may indeed seek to rest here awhile.

Near Bicknoller, West Somerset Railway: front locomotive, Class 25 D7523 *John F. Kennedy* with, to its rear 'Warship' Class 42 D832 *Onslaught*, the latter on loan from the East Lancs Railway, hauling the 18.00 Bishops Lydeard to Williton goods train, 14 June 2008.

It may all look very interesting, as double-headed trains featuring demonstration freights within the preserved scene are a rare event, but D832 *Onslaught* was not in power as it had suffered a failure in coolant supply earlier in the day. Therefore we can't really describe it as 'double-headed' for only one locomotive is in power. The train consist is somewhat eclectic but adds interest to this scene set close to the Quantock hills, with their gentle slopes and woodland proving less austere than nearby Exmoor with its comparatively barren features. Residents of the white-painted house can enjoy 'a room with a view' from whichever window they gaze.

Nethercott, West Somerset Railway: 'Hymek' Class 35 D7076, preserved at the East Lancashire Railway, hauling the 15.40 Minehead to Bishops Lydeard, 16 June 2007.

Here, just on the edge of the Quantocks, the sublime scenery is enjoyed by the passengers as much as the hydraulic hum of the 'Hymek' locomotive is enjoyed by the enthusiasts in the front carriage as it starts its descent towards its destination. Characterised by tranquil woodland, wet meadows, burbling brooks and red soil, it's an area of outstanding beauty noted for many wildflowers, butterflies and birds of prey. Country lanes and stony tracks see plenty of horse riders and walkers and, of course, intrepid photographers exploring interesting locations for their photographs and video cameras. Truly serene surroundings for all who visit this wonderful panoply of unspoilt nature.

Roebuck Farm, West Somerset Railway: 'Hymek' Class 35 D7017, preserved at the West Somerset Railway, hauls the 12.05 Norton Fitzwarren to Minehead non-stop service, 14 June 2009.

The gate in the foreground is a reminder of the foot-crossing at this location. Approaching trains descending from Crowcombe tend to take their speed cautiously as they must negotiate a steady curve, while anybody intending to cross must check before crossing to establish if there is a train approaching – they can usually hear the train from a distance as the sound resounds around the valley. The BR blue livery looks smart although readers may prefer the version of early BR blue with a small yellow panel – or even the two-tone green seen in the previous photograph of this locomotive taken at Washford Bank. The late 1960s and early 1970s must have been a very interesting time during which these transitions of livery were revealed by BR.

Roebuck Farm, West Somerset Railway: 'Warship' Class 42 D832 *Onslaught* on loan from the East Lancashire Railway hauls the 13.40 from Bishops Lydeard to Minehead, 14 June 2009.

In addition to the variations of green and blue livery that appeared during the era of transition from steam to diesel and electric, there was also maroon livery with the small yellow front panels, as seen in the previous photograph of 'Warship' D821 *Greyhound* (p. 119), and this version, with full-front yellow. When all are presented within railway preservation adorned in such immaculate paintwork, it can be difficult to decide which is most preferred, and such will necessarily be a subjective decision, but one does wonder which looked best under the grime of everyday running and weathering. Modellers sometimes add realism to their models by adding these characteristics, for the true railway environment is not correctly presented by this sterile, clean, ultra glossy image. Still, it makes for a pleasant photograph taken while basking in the glorious West Somerset landscape.

Opposite: Crowcombe Heathfield, West Somerset Railway: Class 37 D6737, preserved at South Devon Railway, approaches with the 11.50 Minehead to Bishops Lydeard, 14 June 2008.

Demonstrating full early BR green livery, as here carried by D6737, this green goddess certainly draws attention to the praiseworthy restoration efforts of the Devon Diesel Society. This locomotive was allocated initially to BR Eastern Region, then in the early 1980s it was transferred to and became part of Glasgow Eastfield's allocation for use on the West Highland line. Climbing such gradients as seen here would therefore have been a regular occurrence. The locomotive is near the top of the grade and the English Electric motors can be given a deserved rest – along with the eardrums of the enthusiasts clearly enjoying the 'music'.

Below: Crowcombe Heathfield, West Somerset Railway : 'Hymek' Class 35 D7017, preserved at the West Somerset Railway, hauling the 14.40 Minehead to Bishops Lydeard, 14 June 2009.

The rolling hills of the Quantocks command a steady climb at 1 in 68 from just after Stogumber before slackening to 1 in 100 towards Crowcombe Heathfield station, and the 'Hymek' locomotive emerges from the shadows to salute the completion of the most demanding section of the eastbound climb from Williton. At this location, with all the vivid greens of early summer, the BR blue livery actually adds to the impression made by the train as it scrambles into the sunshine, whereas the two-tone green livery may have struggled to stand out in such circumstances.

Crowcombe Heathfield, West Somerset Railway: 'Western' Class 52 D1062 *Western Courier*, preserved at the Severn Valley Railway, arrives with the 09.05 from Minehead to Bishops Lydeard, 14 June 2009.

Western Courier wore this maroon livery with small yellow panels from May 1963 until October 1968 after which it received blue livery with full yellow ends. Seen in this idyllic setting, with fine weather to match, it is understandable why many consider this livery the best to have adorned the 'Westerns'. Certainly it enhances the graceful curvature and sleek lines of the locomotive, and a throng of dedicated enthusiasts are thoroughly enjoying the characteristic song that is provided by the Maybach engines as they supply the necessary power to ascend the grade.

Crowcombe Heathfield, West Somerset Railway: Class 33 D6566, 33048, preserved at the West Somerset Railway, hauling an early evening Bishops Lydeard to Minehead ballast train, 16 June 2007.

Carefully preserved stations such as here are often bestowed with favourite features such as milk churns, waiting room canopies, flower displays in hanging baskets and traditional metallic adverts (one being for a childhood favourite of mine, Tizer), which all help to provide the atmosphere that enhances the heritage context of the preserved railway scene. It contributes a reflective peace to this location where there are occasional times when trains pass here and all is busy before each of the trains departs and the tranquillity returns to such a rural retreat. The glint off the locomotive draws attention to the low sunlight which bathes the trees in a pleasant summer evening's warmth at the end of the day.

Between Crowcombe and Stogumber, West Somerset Railway: Class 14 locomotives with, front, D9520 preserved at the Nene Valley Railway and 'second' D9526 preserved at the West Somerset Railway, hauling the 10.05 Minehead to Bishops Lydeard, Saturday 14 June 2008.

Certainly these locomotives look smart as a pair working together in their BR green livery with the yellow front panel embellished with 'wasp stripes' required for their daily toil in the yards between which they worked their short distance trip freights. Those large window cabs provided excellent all-round visibility which further facilitated such work. Their short life working on BR Western and Eastern Regions was curtailed not – as was occasionally the case with the early diesel designs introduced in the 1960s – as a result of unreliability but because the type of duties to which they were assigned saw rapid contraction. Originally all were allocated to British Railways Western Region, but in January 1967 twenty were sent to Hull (Dairycoates) on the Eastern Region followed by a further batch later that same year. There they proved inadequate for their intended duties at Hull docks and were soon stored. Many found further work with either the National Coal Board (NCB) or the British Steel Corporation (BSC). To have found one working in these delightful sylvan surroundings would have been a rare treat indeed.

Approaching Corfe Viaduct, Swanage Railway: Class 33 33012, D6515 with a train for Swanage, 1 April 2006.

A pleasant tribute to the era of Southern green with a typical passenger train working that might have occurred on a non-electrified section of the Southern network, most of which was equipped with third rail. The white wrap-around in this specific livery distinguished the cab of this versatile locomotive. When first encountered on a trip from my then northern home which took me behind a Class 33 on the section from Basingstoke southwards with the Liverpool to Bournemouth through working, I was most impressed by the power, acceleration and lively character of the locomotive; my bias for the heavy duty northern diesels was indeed challenged! I particularly liked the distinctive sound of the Sulzer engine with its Crompton and Parkinson traction motors, which was echoed in the nickname 'Cromptons' given by the enthusiast community.

Corfe Castle Station, Swanage Railway: Class 47/4 47635 *The Lass O' Ballochmyle*, preserved on the Swanage Railway, hauls a late afternoon Swanage to Norden service, 11 May 2008.

A short climb up the grassy slopes below Corfe Castle is rewarded by this fine vista over the station as it nestles close to the surrounding picture postcard Dorset cottages and countryside. The careful restoration of the site to an authentic two-platform countryside station is remarkable when compared to photographs from the days just after closure when the rails were hastily removed in July 1972 by an unsympathetic BR. Heavy Class 47 locomotives passing through would not have been the first thing on the mind of the preservationists; without their efforts and determination, gala events featuring a multitude of diesel or steam locomotives, for which the Swanage Railway has earned a praiseworthy respect, simply would never have taken place.

Corfe Common, Swanage Railway: 'Deltic' Class 55 55022 *Royal Scots Grey*, preserved at the East Lancashire Railway, hauls the 13.50 Norden to Swanage, 9 May 2009.

An East Coast Main Line locomotive passing below the Purbeck Hills and crossing Corfe Common – well, in preservation, we can allow such travesties! Like the Class 52 'Westerns', the 'Deltics' have earned a place in railway history and draw significant crowds of enthusiastic fans. This was also the case during the steam to diesel transition era when steam-only die-hard photographers were content to record their duties on camera. Judging by the exhaust emissions, it looks as if both the Napier engines are in operation, although the climb up to Harmans Cross is brief. Heads out of open windows and a full train proves the popularity of these locomotives.

Above: Corfe Common, Swanage Railway: Class 20 20188, D8188 crosses Corfe Common with an afternoon train for Swanage, 1 April 2006.

This picture could be entitled 'The Black Marauder', for this black-liveried Class 20 appears on scene as if carrying out a raid while passing below the Purbeck Hills. After all, locally, contraband was landed from large fishing boats and from luggers. Nearby Studland Bay was particularly popular, because it was free of dangerous rocks and has a safe, sandy bottom, and also because Studland itself was very isolated. This was often only a temporary resting place for the Purbeck smugglers. Their goods would have been shipped onwards by sea because the option of taking goods directly overland was too risky, since the land routes off the island were carefully guarded.

The exposed barren grasses are still pale and thin after a cold winter, though enjoying the gentle warming from the spring sunshine that this peninsula enjoys.

Opposite: Corfe Common, Swanage Railway: Class 47/4 47635 *The Lass O' Ballochmyle*, preserved on the Swanage Railway, hauling the 13.30 Norden to Harmans Cross, 11 May 2008.

Springtime blossom in supreme splendour salutes ex-Scottish Sulzer! As with many railway locations, catching the wonders of spring's tapestry of rich colours can be challenging depending on whether there has been clearance of vegetation in cuttings and alongside the rails (essential for purposes of protecting the permanent way). Where possible I try to incorporate the wild flowers and colours although I leave the viewer to imagine the sounds of the bees pollinating, grass being mowed, a gentle breeze blowing in the trees and, of course, the sound of the approaching train.

Corfe Common, Swanage Railway: Class 45 45060 *Sherwood Forester*, preserved at Barrow Hill, departs Corfe Castle with the 11.50 Norden to Swanage, 9 May 2009.

'Peak' locomotives became a reliable workhorse in from the 1960s to the 1980s when they hauled the main line expresses emanating from London St Pancras to destinations along the Midland Railway – including the Settle and Carlisle line, and also over the demanding TransPennine routes from Liverpool to Newcastle. They were also a familiar sight along the North Wales coast and on cross country services from the north-east to the south-west. Alongside such versatility, they impressed with their performance and were best suited to the long distances demanded of them. For these reasons they are among the classes of diesel that have attracted a cult following, and their appearance at diesel galas is always welcomed. The incorporation of split head code boxes at the outside edges of the locomotive's nose front indicates a design intention to use gangway doors, but one that was not as widely applied as first expected.

With its equally impressive historical record, Corfe Castle, built in 1280 in the reign of King Edward I, competes for attention, albeit for entirely different reasons. It is an evocative and captivating ruin which saw use both as a royal residence and as a garrison. Considered one of the most extravagant and formidable castles for its time it was one of the first to be constructed using stone, in this case limestone from the local hills.

Corfe Common, Swanage Railway: Class 45 45060 *Sherwood Forester*, preserved at Barrow Hill, heads the 17.30 Norden to Swanage. At rear is Class 33 33111, preserved at the Swanage Railway. Class 117 Pressed Steel diesel multiple units 51346 and 51388 are formed within the train consist, Saturday 9 May 2009.

A late afternoon view of the same 'Peak' locomotive with the distant outline of Corfe Castle exuding its presence as a memorial towards all who defended and protected the locality, sometimes at the cost to their lives. The locomotive looks entirely at home amidst the local rolling hills, helping to recall its own heady days climbing through the demanding gradients of the Peak District in all seasons and weathers. The split head code boxes add a favourite feature of these locomotives and the BR blue is captured to perfection. The somewhat mixed rake of rolling stock reminds us that preserved railways must call on their full resources to supply the demands of popular diesel galas which attract enthusiasts from far and wide.

Above: Corfe Common, Swanage Railway: Class 47/4 47635 *The Lass O' Ballochmyle*, at the rear of the 14.25 Harmans Cross to Norden. Isle of Purbeck hills in background, 11 May 2008.

Allocated to Haymarket Depot, Edinburgh, this Class 47 spent much of its time in Scotland as one of the sub Class 47/6 that was created for Scottish sleeper workings (within Scotland). Enjoying the full light of day, it is here working one of the shorter paths to and from Norden, where there is ample parking. This is the halfway point of the preserved line at Harmans Cross which suggests why there appear to be relatively few travelling passengers, as the majority of non-rail enthusiasts will by now be enjoying the late spring warmth at the seaside town of Swanage. Even the nearby main road will be enjoying a breather before the late afternoon return home by car to the conurbations of Poole and Bournemouth gets underway and clogs up entirely while negotiating its way through Corfe. No gridlock, however, on this railway.

Opposite: Corfe Common, Swanage Railway: Class 33 33012, D6515 hauls a late afternoon train towards Corfe Common and Corfe Castle station, 1 April 2006.

'Crompton contemplates Corfe Castle while considering this classic semaphore signal in this Southern soliloquy.' How's that for a tongue-twister? We could well be on a Southern Railway byway in the BR 1960s era with very little visible to date the scene pictured as actually taken in the twenty-first century. Such scenes are increasingly difficult to capture, because a modern car or lorry might be passing over the road bridge at the same time as the train passes below. The lineside hut adds further to the atmosphere, especially as it is constructed from concrete once so typically used by the Southern.

Shackerstone, the Battlefield Railway: Class 33 33053 arrives from Shenton, seen passing a Midland Railway signal box ex-Measham, 28 October 2007.

Autumn's golden hues nearly always add a seasonal depth of colour to railway landscapes, especially where there are deciduous trees in abundance. The dark threatening sky here indicates a heavy rain shower is on the way, which will bring down some of those colourful leaves onto the railway line. Normally that spells problems for main line railway operators, who have to deal with the leafy mulch deposited on the rails, and can even mean signallers cannot detect a train's location. It's a significant challenge for Network Rail which claims that there are 10 million trees on and next to the railway in Britain! All this is efficiently cleared away by the railhead treatment trains (RHTTs) which clear the railheads by spraying them with a water jet at very high pressure.

Toddington, Gloucestershire and Warwickshire Railway: in the cutting north of Toddington Class 24 24081, preserved at Gloucestershire and Warwickshire Railway, awaits departure with ballast wagons, 5 April 2008.

This class of locomotive looked very much at home in BR blue livery, here applied with genuine authenticity. The Class 24s were very much part of the north-west railway scene in which I grew up, with freight diagrams taking them to various parts of Lancashire, Cheshire and North Wales. While not exactly overpowered, they performed their often mundane duties with efficiency and quiet determination. These locomotives used white discs to signify the train type and the one shown here would have been accurate for a ballast train. Where operated on preserved railways, demonstration freight trains are welcomed by railway photographers as they offer something different while providing a valued and memorable recollection of this aspect of historic railway operations.

Toddington, Gloucestershire and Warwickshire Railway: Class 20 20137, preserved at Gloucestershire and Warwickshire Railway, in a light engine move, 5 April 2008.

Plenty of interest here can be found in the way of atmosphere added by the fire buckets, lineside hut, water tower, tank wagons and distant station platform. The permanent way looks well used, enhancing the concept of this as a 'working' railway. Even the locomotive looks as if the paintwork has become partly bestowed with a layer of grime. Class 20s would have operated in very similar railway landscapes in the 1960s when some of them would also have carried this BR green livery with a small yellow panel. Their duties as freight locomotives would have taken them to destinations where muck and grime were inevitably part of the everyday scene, and this aspect of realism is sometimes lost when preserved locomotives appear in resplendent spotless condition.

Toddington, Gloucestershire and Warwickshire Railway: Class 24 24081, preserved at Gloucestershire and Warwickshire Railway, in a light engine movement, 5 April 2008.

A scene hinting at the complex thread of interweaving lines dividing or meeting at a classic railway junction found alongside a diesel stabling point in the days of BR blue livery. It suggests a date sometime in the 1970s when semaphore signals were still predominant away from the main lines. This is what keeps the preservation sector interesting – the ability to honour the era of steam and diesel with all the various aspects of accompanying heritage features which combine to recreate scenes that provide much interest to rail enthusiasts who experienced 'the real thing' in its heyday. Here the disc head codes indicate the locomotive has just come off an express freight train partly fitted and with automatic braking operating on not less than half the vehicles. While a fictional working on a preserved railway it is a further aspect of detail which enhances the authenticity of the railway landscape recalled.

Near Bewdley, Severn Valley Railway: 'Western' Class 52 D1013 *Western Ranger* descends from Foley Park tunnel with a mid-afternoon train from Kidderminster to Bridgnorth, 15 October 2005.

    The autumnal gold and yellow of the embankment complements the full yellow end livery of this Western in BR blue livery. This colour scheme was – and remains – very popular with 'Western' aficionados who will probably be able to supply you with the dates of the different liveries worn by each member of the class. The locomotive has even been used in driver experience courses, which are exhilarating events considering you can fully power those Maybach engines while under supervision in the cab. We must leave the exhilarating sound emitted to the reader's imagination. Here, we can but pause to admire its aesthetic appeal, to study the detail, to reminisce, to contemplate its place in modern preservation, its continuing role within the railway landscape. In this we must thank the railway preservationists for enabling such an unrivalled contribution to honouring the railway landscapes of the UK.

Chapter 4
THE PRESERVED STEAM RAILWAYS LANDSCAPE

Buckfastleigh, South Devon Railway: left is GWR 5600 Class 0-6-2T 6695, stabled, having arrived in loop with empty coaching stock. It is preserved at the Swanage Railway. Right is GWR 4500 Class 2-6-2T 5526 in a light engine shunting movement, preserved at the South Devon Railway, 12 April 2009.

An interesting 'Devon duo' separated by a key ingredient of the preserved railway scene: the water tank. There's one at Totnes too – and watching the locomotive crew busy filling their steeds with the life-essence of water always draws a fascinated crowd. When the water overflows and the job is complete, it is then that the crew can take a short break before their next turn; 6695 may well have completed its duties for the day but 5526 looks ready to take another turn. Sharp-eyed observers will note the interesting collection of historic cars in the right-hand background – they are part of an extra display on this Easter Sunday.

Buckfastleigh, South Devon Railway: GWR 4500 Class 2-6-2T 5526 arrives with the 16.30 from Totnes, 12 October 2008.

The golden colours of the autumn trees are bathed in the glow of a late afternoon sun and the footbridge pays tribute to such in its own similar colour scheme. Even the hue of signal box red brick wishes to join in this welcome splash of colour! A journey along the previously named 'Dart Valley Railway' is special at this time of year for it accompanies the river for its length and the trees along the route are clothed in a rich canopy of yellow, orange and red. The Great Western brown of the coaching stock blends in too – nature and transport combine for a memorable display, enhanced by a seasonal celebration before the nights draw in and the onset of winter arrives.

Near Caddaford, South Devon Railway: GWR 5600 Class 0-6-2T 6695, preserved at the Swanage Railway, hauls the 09.50 Buckfastleigh to Totnes mixed freight, 11 April 2009.

This demonstration freight, run as part of the South Devon Railway's Anniversary Gala celebrating 40 years since the reopening of the former Ashburton branch, has yet to pull away, hence the simple wisp of smoke just evident. It's a wonderful collection of wagons including a china clay example with its blue tarpaulin and, at the back, several milk tanks. At least two brake vans are contained in the mix. This motley collection would, in steam days, have been collected from the wayside halts en route to the next railway yard where there would be further shunting with plenty of clanking and raised voices calling on the various movements needed. The whole set is marvellously clean and freshly painted, whereas in the everyday world of steam-hauled freight, grime and dirt would reflect the mundane nature of the conditions many such wagons would display. It's a great tribute to that era when such trains were commonplace throughout the land. Block container trains just don't possess the same character.

Above: Caddaford Curve, South Devon Railway: GWR 4500 Class 2-6-2T 5526 accelerates the 10.45 Buckfastleigh to Totnes Riverside past Caddaford Curve alongside the River Dart, 2 January 2010.

No wonder that the lure of the spectacular steam locomotive hissing and chuffing while exhausting volcanic eruptions of steam on a winter's morning draws out the photographers at any of the nation's preserved steam railways. The very soul and life of the beast is fully on show for all to see, though the fireman has had to work very hard to help the engine give its magnificent display. Both driver and fireman deserve our congratulations for such a splendid expression of power and might.

Opposite above: Caddaford Curve, South Devon Railway: GWR 4500 Class 2-6-2T 5526 hauls the 10.45 Buckfastleigh to Totnes Riverside, 2 January 2010.

Winter's low sunlight glints off the Great Western brake compartment coach behind the locomotive as it pulls hard away from the curve and leaves a billowing blast of uplifted steam vapour trailing into the cold air. Passengers are snug and warm from the steam heating, no doubt thankful that none of which is escaping. The train exerts an intention to climb towards its destination implicit in the hills ahead, though in fact the line keeps to the valley as it hugs the nearby River Dart. We are warmly welcomed aboard to join it on our journey through the preserved steam landscape.

Opposite below: Near Caddaford, South Devon Railway: GWR 4500 Class 2-6-2T 5552 hauling the 11.35 Buckfastleigh to Totnes, 11 April 2009.

With a view towards Dartmoor's rolling hills at the back of Ashburton, we enjoy the spectacle of steam in Devon's springtime flourish. Ashburton station was closed to passengers in 1958 but freight lingered until 1962. The building in 1971 of the A38 dual carriageway across the route north of Buckfastleigh meant that no future return for trains to Ashburton could be possible, hence the present site at Buckfastleigh provides the terminus station for the South Devon Railway's steam trains. Renewed power lines are the only real indication that this picture isn't taken in the golden age of the GWR branch line. Daily steam trains from March to October help keep such a memory well and truly alive.

Near Hood Bridge, South Devon Railway: GWR 4500 Class 2-6-2T 5526 hauls a mid-afternoon milk train from Bishops Bridge to Buckfastleigh, 4 April 2010.

Here's a reminder that milk trains were a way of life for much of the steam era, and Devon's rural creameries helped to supply the good citizens of the cities with their daily dairy needs. The image captures this key ingredient of the Great Western branch line, just as the milk conveyed is an integral part of the morning breakfast cereal and cup of tea that are so eagerly consumed at the start of each day. The locomotive potters along at the speed permitted for the country branch line, being in no rush for such a train returning the empty milk tanks for replenishment. Once the tanks have been filled, a sense of greater urgency will be needed to hurry the milk for the longer journey back up the main line for its distribution to the homes of suburbia.

Hood Bridge, South Devon Railway: 'Britannia' Class 7MT 4-6-2 70013 *Oliver Cromwell* hauls the 14.17 Totnes to Buckfastleigh, 4 April 2010.

A giant of steam, a little out of place along a small branch line, but who cares? Certainly not the photographers who have come to admire such a spectacular star of main line magnificence. The locomotive had on the previous day hauled an excursion, 'The Royal Duchy', operated by the Railway Touring Company, down into Cornwall and had run up light engine in the morning to the South Devon Railway from St Blazey, where it had rested overnight. Devon would have been a long way from its usual racing grounds on the Great Eastern lines and in fact it started its working life at Norwich Shed. This 'Britannia' was one of the fleet that revolutionised Great Eastern main line schedules in the 1950s.

Hood Bridge, South Devon Railway: LMS Class 5MT 4-6-0 44871 *Sovereign* hauls a late afternoon service from Buckfastleigh to Totnes.

Two for the price of one! This locomotive had also worked in tandem with the 'Britannia' on 'The Royal Duchy' tour referred to in the previous photograph. With a locomotive weight of 72 tons and a tender weight of 53, although lighter than the Britannia (94 tons), she can still be described as a heavyweight for such a rural light branch. Even so, it all looks very much the part as she cautiously approaches the lower quadrant signal showing a clear road ahead for Bishops Bridge and Staverton. The River Dart is at a high level after spring rain has increased the flow in the many tributaries that flow into the Dart from nearby Dartmoor. The immaculate permanent way reveals much care and effort from the track maintenance department on this railway with its strong volunteer force. The dappled light plays hide-and-seek with the shadows of the branches which reach out to see this spectacle for themselves.

Hood Bridge, South Devon Railway: GWR 4500 Class 2-6-2T 5526 passes alongside the River Dart with a mid-afternoon train to Buckfastleigh, 23 March 2008.

Looking very much the 'branch line scene', a genuine Great Western locomotive and accompanying carmine and cream carriage set accelerate away from Bishops Bridge. The preservation steam railway scene in Britain is varied in its attempts to guarantee authenticity, but the South Devon Railway certainly excels in such. The very high percentage of volunteer support in all aspects of the running of the railway is reflected in the high level of commitment and shared desire to provide the very best travel experience for the many passengers who seek out a journey along the line.

Above: Staverton, South Devon Railway: GWR 4500 Class 2-6-2T 5526 passes with the 11.30 Totnes Riverside to Buckfastleigh on a cool winter's morning, 2 January 2010.

The diffused sunlight plays hide and seek with the shadows of the branches as cascades of light creep across the foreground of this tranquil scene to where the locomotive pulls away from a signal check, no doubt after waiting for the up train to arrive at Bishops Bridge on the far side of Staverton station. This down train has priority in setting down its passengers at the single platform before departing towards Buckfastleigh. They may well choose to walk past here as they follow the riverside along its winding course in the clear air and calm of such a winter's day.

Opposite: Near Staverton, South Devon Railway: 9400 Class 0-6-0PT 9466 evokes memories of branch line steam alongside the River Dart as it passes through a spring glade where the colour reflects the grace of the loco and matching coaches, 10 April 2019.

The branch line from Totnes to Ashburton was primarily a line for freight, carrying agricultural feeds, timber for joinery and wagons of coal. Many such lines relied on similar merchandise for paying their way, and passenger trains were a secondary contributor to the main business. Now the line relies entirely on the revenue provided by the tourists: coach parties, school groups, steam train enthusiasts and many families who join the trains for a journey alongside the River Dart. They partake in the history of the line as they travel along its original route hauled by a restored steam locomotive, and all the many photographs that they take – whether on a mobile phone or the latest digital SLR camera – create their own history of the occasion when they journeyed back in time to experience the authentic steam experience.

Above: Dartington, South Devon Railway: GWR 5600 Class 0-6-2T 6695 hauls the 15.20 Buckfastleigh to Totnes, 12 April 2009.

After spring rains, as demonstrated by the high level of the river, the relatively fast-flowing waters of the Dart prevent a complete reflection but it's there in principle. This type of locomotive had been used extensively in the Welsh Valleys for working coal trains, in particular by the Rhymney, Taff Vale and Barry railways. They were extremely versatile engines with impressive power and acceleration and capable of speeds of 60mph, although they had a tendency to run hot axle boxes. The 0-6-2T looks quite at home in this scenery as it encounters a glade of trees clearly awaiting spring's blossom to emerge, of which there are promising glimpses.

Opposite above: Dartington, South Devon Railway: 9400 Class 0-6-0PT 9466 works hard as it heads towards Totnes along the 'Royal Mile', recreating a genuine riverside branch line scene, 10 April 2019.

Passengers on board the train as it passes near the Dartington estate may not realise the quietly-kept link that this secluded part of the railway line has with royalty. The branch line is connected at Totnes with one of the two main rail routes to the west that existed at the time of World War II, and here was an ideal place to hide a train secretly in a quiet spot. So, it was used to stable the Royal Train overnight so that the royal passengers could then get a peaceful night's sleep. The golden hue of the spring foliage pays its own respects.

Opposite below: Waterside, Torbay, Paignton and Dartmouth Steam Railway: GWR 4073 'Castle' Class 4-6-0 5029 *Nunney Castle* hauling an early afternoon train to Kingswear, 10 May 2009.

It's easy to see why Torbay appeals to visitors. The GWR was fully aware of this in its promotion of the seaside towns of Torquay and Paignton. Passengers on board this service will be able to enjoy the sound of the hard-working locomotive as it ascends the 1 in 71 bank at Waterside and passes the spectacle of Torbay and the beach at Broadsands with its colourful beach huts, and a glimpse towards Brixham to the south. After Greenway tunnel the views towards Dartmouth will be over on the right of the train as it heads towards Kingswear for the ferry link. The air must be cool for there is plenty of steam left in that trail – so perhaps not a day for the beach after all?

Waterside, Torbay, Paignton and Dartmouth Steam Railway: GWR 4200 Class 2-8-0T 4277 *Hercules* hauls a mid-afternoon Paignton to Kingswear train, 10 May 2009.

In the heyday of steam, this branch would have seen GWR 'Castle', 'Manor' and 'Hall' Class locomotives working a variety of trains including the 'Torbay Express' and the 'Devonian' alongside the scenic splendour of Torbay. Now it still sees a 'Manor' (*Lydham Manor*) but also a frequent diet of 2-8-0Ts including *Goliath* and *Hercules*, both examples of a type which was more used to working heavy coal trains in the Welsh Valleys. Yet the names are appropriate for they must need a giant's strength to haul seven carriage trains up the 1 in 71 gradient from Goodrington. The fireman has his work cut out while passengers can relax and admire the fine view that has so appealed to many of their predecessors carried over the route since preservation fortunately saved the line at the end of 1972.

Kingswear, Paignton and Dartmouth Steam Railway: A1 Class 4-6-2 60163 *Tornado* runs light engine after an empty coaching stock movement of the 'Torbay Express', 2 August 2009.

The BR apple green livery first worn by *Tornado* seems to match well the lush green grass and foliage of the West Country to which it has strayed while working the ever-popular 'Torbay Express'. Later in its life, early BR express passenger blue livery was applied which made for an equally appealing decor. Most of the crowds of passengers upon arrival will have headed for the boat crossing over to the honeypot that is Dartmouth, no doubt in search of Devon cream teas, ice cream and fish 'n' chips! However, given that it is a warm day when steam is less evident, *Tornado* provides a fine display for those onlookers who have remained to see the necessary shunting movement by this mighty locomotive once released from the points at the west end of the station.

Above: Kingswear, Paignton and Dartmouth Steam Railway: GWR 5205 Class 2-8-0T 5239 *Goliath* arrives with the 14.15 Paignton to Kingswear, 2 August 2009.

Part of the delight of rolling down into Kingswear by train is the wonderful unwrapping of the unrivalled vista of the River Dart's aquamarine tidal waters, along with the marina and moorings all holding their myriads of yachts and cruisers, canoes and dinghies of multitudinous sizes. Historic Dartmouth can finally be glimpsed across the river as we curve into the terminus at Kingswear station. A special treat may accompany those who depart on the next returning train to Paignton, for the renowned 1924-built coal-fired paddle steamer *Kingswear Castle* often 'coincidentally' times its tours to hiss and chuff alongside, even contributing its own steam whistle to the atmospheric sounds as the locomotive applies maximum effort to climb the steep ascent of Greenway Bank.

Opposite: Kingswear, Paignton and Dartmouth Steam Railway: GWR 4500 Class 2-6-2T 4588 *Trojan* departs towards Britannia Halt with a midday train for Paignton, 17 September 2005.

Those content to pay their supplement in order to travel in the 'Devon Belle' Pullman observation car have the added benefit of hearing the adjacent locomotive working in full steam as it climbs Greenway Bank towards Churston. Previously, they will have travelled at the rear of the train affording an unfolding vista of Torbay as they climbed alongside the small bays and inlets which illustrate the concept of the English Riviera that the Great Western was so keen to promote (alongside the famed Cornish version). The coach was originally built as an ambulance vehicle in 1917, before being converted into a Pullman observation car in 1921. Such carriages operated in lines around England and especially in Scotland, and became known for the distinctive design which offered panoramic views to their enthralled passengers.

Minehead, West Somerset Railway: LMS 7F Class 2-8-0 88 (53808) Fowler design for Somerset and Dorset Joint Railway, with a freight train demonstration, 19 March 2006.

The Prussian blue livery bestowed on this freight locomotive may seem a little extravagant but compared to its authentic unlined black it shows that such application needs not be controversial, for it enhances the scene admirably. Not many preserved lines can provide such a mixed rake of freight wagons and the appeal to steam photographers is increased by the infrequent opportunities for capturing such on camera. It is particularly welcome when it is provided for more than just photo-charter participants, as indeed was the case here at Minehead.

Viewed over the Bristol Channel from Conygar Wood: GWR 6000 Class 6024 *King Edward I* hauls a train approaching Dunster from Minehead to Bishops Lydeard, 27 March 2010.

The 'King' Class were relatively heavy locomotives, best known for tightly scheduled main line express trains in their heyday. The preserved steam railway can entertain such finely restored examples as long as the speed limits are adhered to, and the permanent way well maintained; this train poses little threat as it ambles towards nearby Dunster station. The Bristol Channel is a little choppy and there is a haze which disguises the South Wales coast which is visible in the distance on a clear day. The tanker keeps close to the coast, ignorant of the train's proceedings and the golfers' attention is diverted by the desire to complete their game successfully as they draw off the tee and apply the requisite strength of mind and determination along with the best stance and posture. The locomotive crew will need similar resolve and skill soon as they must face the challenge of climbing towards the Quantocks in their journey towards Bishops Lydeard.

Blue Anchor, West Somerset Railway: 7F Class 2-8-0 ... 88 (53808)... hauling the 17.30 Minehead to Bishops Lydeard, 24 March 2007.

The late afternoon sunset glints off both locomotive and coaches as the final train of the day heads towards its ultimate destination. Gently pulling towards Blue Anchor, there is no urgency sensed in this journey through such a calm and tranquil scene. The telegraph poles and semaphore signal help to recreate the atmosphere as they provide their own salute to a tapestry which facilitates any fading memories of steam with a soupçon of authenticity and recollection.

Washford, West Somerset Railway: Peckett R3 Class 0-4-0ST 1788 *Kilmersdon* in shunting demonstrations with mixed-freight and bogie flat-wagon mounted milk tanks in the Somerset and Dorset Museum railway sidings, 21 March 2009.

For an industrial shunting locomotive built in 1929 which spent its life at Kilmersdon Colliery, North Somerset, this locomotive is in fine fettle as its glossy coat of paint and expressive head of steam reveal. It's a busy scene with the driver paying careful attention to the jostling wagons as they are moved along the short sidings and past the station platform. The private owner wagons, including the crane, all add to the atmosphere of the hustle and bustle that was to be found disturbing the peace at rural stations, many of which came equipped with loading bays and goods sheds. Such was unfortunately all lost as the alternative lure of modern road transport and improved roads discouraged such time-consuming procedures, fortunately revived if briefly by this worthy recreation of a truly bygone era.

Opposite: Williton, West Somerset Railway: West Country Pacific 4-6-2 34046 *Braunton* recalls a 1960s scene as it leans into the curve approaching Williton en route from Minehead to Bishops Lydeard and passes Class 47 D1661, 27 March 2010.

Pure nostalgia! The BR lined green with late crest livery applied to *Braunton* perfectly mirrors the BR green of the stabled Class 47. Both look superb as they authentically complement each other and illustrate a narrative in the value of liveries embellishing and adorning preserved locomotives. In fact, both are so clean and shining that it belies the fact that they would have indeed been covered in a layer of grime during their original working days prior to preservation. The subsequent BR blue was pleasant and suited some locomotives particularly well, but 'everything' without divergence carried the same blue so that it became ubiquitous. BR green is therefore seen by many to be the jewel in the crown of 1960s liveries, and its transient rule was only challenged by some exceptions such as the 1960s Nanking blue applied to the specialist luxury express 'Blue Pullman' diesel trains.

Below: Castle Hill, West Somerset Railway: LMS Class 5MT 'Black 5' 4-6-0 45231 *The Sherwood Forester* hauling the 11.10 Minehead to Bishops Lydeard, 21 March 2009.

Castle Hill provides an excellent backdrop for both steam and diesel locomotives as they commence their long climb from the Somerset coast towards the Quantock Hills. The sound of the steady pulse of the exhaust and sheer strain of effort applied by the locomotive is reinforced by the trail of steam forced upwards as, like the locomotive, it reaches out in its ascent to its highest goal. Here is truly a shared exhilarating experience for the photographers, passengers and locomotive crew alike.

Near Bicknoller, West Somerset Railway: West Country Pacific 4-6-2 34046 *Braunton* passes below the Quantock Hills bathed in late December's hues, 28 December 2008.

The autumnal bronze and gold of the ferns and bracken carpeting the nearby Quantock Hills is enhanced by the gentle glow of a winter afternoon's receding sunlight. The sheep graze on as if undisturbed by the train which, given the season, is no doubt carrying contented families out for a festive journey down the line served by a host of volunteers conveying mince pies and a warming punch – or cider, for we are in Somerset! The immaculate condition of the locomotive is a tribute to the commitment and hard work applied, no doubt in a labour of love, by a separate team of dedicated volunteers while it has resided 'on shed' at Minehead – the splendid glint's perfect reflection provides a very worthwhile reward.

Near East Combe, between Crowcombe and Bishops Lydeard, West Somerset Railway: Front locomotive is Fowler design LMS Class 4F 0-6-0 44422, and second is Stanier design LMS Class 5MT 2-6-0 42968 hauling an afternoon service from Bishops Lydeard to Minehead, 6 October 2007.

The chill of the cool early autumn air and steady gradient enables this volcanic display to be admired, if not relished, at its best. The cacophony of sound can be imagined as the two locomotives in tandem rise to their challenge, each with its own exhaust beat and hiss of venting steam. The shattered peace will soon return, but the sound of the train as it climbs further towards Crowcombe will resound for quite some time afterwards, as it continues to be echoed off the nearby hills. The lucky punters on board will no doubt have all possible windows fully open, regardless of any draught created – and who can blame them.

Approaching Roebuck Gate level crossing, West Somerset Railway: Front locomotive is GWR 4500 Class 2-6-2T 5553, preserved at the West Somerset Railway, and second is GWR 4500 Class 2-6-2T 5521, preserved at the Dean Forest Railway, with the 14.20 Minehead to Bishops Lydeard, 24 March 2007.

The permanent way hut reminds us that much work is needed to maintain the preserved railway's permanent way, which is certainly taking a pounding here as these 'Small Prairie' Class locomotives upwardly belch steam and smoke as they slog up the 1 in 100 gradient towards Crowcombe. Their long and relentless climb from Williton will soon be crested once they reach Crowcombe Heathfield station, and both driver and fireman can then breathe a sigh of relief. Passengers on the train can, until then, enjoy the steady surge and sound of these powerful locomotives as it echoes around the woodland through which the train emerges, intent on defeating the challenge of the climb.

Roebuck Farm, West Somerset Railway: GWR 2884 Class 2-8-0 3850 operating the 11.35 Bishops Lydeard to Minehead, 28 December 2008.

A winter's scene welcomed by clear blue skies and the remnants of an overnight frost. The late morning sun bathes the scene in the gentle light that characterises the very short daylight at year's end, and the air is cold and crisp. There is little steam as the train is on its descent from Crowcombe and the loco crew have time to look at the passing scenery while the passengers on board are more than likely enjoying a mince pie and a cup of mulled wine. Most preserved railways provide such a service during the Christmas season and trains are generally well loaded, thus helping to finance the railway's operations during the forthcoming winter shut-down once the holidays are finished.

Above: Approaching Corfe Viaduct, Swanage Railway: BR Class 4MT 2-6-4T 80078 with a demonstration freight train, 1 April 2006.

A favourite for photographers of preserved steam railways is the mixed freight. Modern European railways operate mostly block trains, having the same type of merchandise, be it timber, cement, limestone, quarried stone, china clay or – now significantly reduced – coal. The ubiquitous container trains form the majority of fast freight, and the 'stack' trains of the US take this concept to the limit with double-stacked containers on half-mile long trains. The unfitted branch line freight, with its miscellany of types and colours of wagon that is sometimes provided for visitors to preserved lines' special events, offers a reminder of the local freight scene - unhurried, clattering along with some sense of timeless purpose as the contents are conveyed to the expectant merchant awaiting its arrival at the goods siding or warehouse.

Opposite: Approaching Corfe Viaduct, Swanage Railway: BR Class 4MT 2-6-4T 80078 leads GWR Class 5600 0-6-2T 6695 with a late afternoon train from Norden to Swanage as it approaches Corfe Viaduct, 1 April 2006.

A colourful duo add their own splash of steam to the surroundings as they pull away from Norden on a cool spring afternoon. The billowing steam catches its breath as it is whisked away into the ether, joining to form a swirling mass of pure white. The winter's landscape is bereft of signs of springtime, the barren branches and faded green grass here enjoying a short glimpse of weak sunshine before the chill of the forthcoming cold night arrives.

Above: Approaching Corfe Viaduct, Swanage Railway: BR Class 4MT 2-6-4T 80078 departs Norden with the 12.11 Norden to Swanage, 1 April 2006.

The cool air enhances the emission of steam which has been caught by the stiff westerly breeze on this early spring day. The freshly painted maroon carriage at the front reminds us that not all trains on the Somerset and Dorset Railway were green liveried Southern stock, for the Bradford to Bournemouth trains and excursions from the Midlands in the early BR era generally featured stock wearing maroon or LMS 'Crimson Lake' livery. Appropriately the stock is hauled by a BR locomotive built at Brighton in 1954. It's certainly working hard to move its load on the approach to Corfe Viaduct.

Opposite above: Corfe Castle, Swanage Railway: JZ Yugoslavia Class 62 0-6-0T 30075 (preserved at the East Somerset Railway) departs from Corfe station. At rear is BR Class 4MT 2-6-4T 80104, 7 July 2007.

The Yugoslavian-built Class 62 US type 0-6-0 tank steam locomotive looks entirely at home with its Southern Railway black livery. It has been modified to resemble a Southern Railway USA Class – such locomotives saw service in the UK, including fourteen on the Southern Railway. Providing a shuttle service from Harman's Cross, it needs little effort to haul the short train away, especially as 80104 appears to be doing most of the work as it pushes from the back. Residents of the adjacent Dorset cottages need to be rail enthusiasts if they are to tolerate the regular gaze of the passing passengers and the smuts of steam landing on their washing while it is drying outside.

Opposite below: Corfe Castle, Swanage Railway: GWR Class 5600 0-6-2T 6695 arrives at Corfe Castle station with an early afternoon train for Swanage, 10 September 2006.

This Dorset scene is complemented by the fine cottage below the embankment and by the frame provided by the semaphore signals which govern the entrance to and exit from the loop at Corfe Castle station. The coaches may be Southern green but the parched grasses of Challow Hill suggest that there has not been any rain for several weeks during the hot summer. The exhaust fumes of 6695 similarly struggle to be noticed as they vaporise in the heat of the day. For those needing a replenishing drink and who have time to relax between photographing the arrivals and departures within the busy timetable, there is a very pleasant beer garden just out of sight to the left.

Corfe Castle, Swanage Railway: GWR Class 5600 0-6-2T 6695 leads BR Class 4MT 2-6-4T 80078 as they depart Corfe Castle station with an afternoon train bound for Norden, 1 April 2006.

Northbound trains departing Corfe Castle gaze down on the gardens and rooftops of the properties backing onto the line. The inhabitants must surely enjoy rather than endure the sound of a pair of locomotives working in tandem and creating voluminous steam as they pull away from the station. The contrast in liveries is interesting and complementary, with different BR emblems. The 'lion on wheel' totem carried by 80078 recalls the heraldic imagery of mediaeval armies, here placed on a spoked locomotive wheel. More elaborate was the later 'lion and silver wheel' crest as featured on 6695 which showed a heraldic crown of gold on which are arranged the rose (for England), the thistle (for Scotland), the leek (for Wales) and the oak leaf (for all Great Britain). It is interesting that a cast aluminium version of this was attached to the electric blue locomotives introduced to the West Coast Main Line in the early 1960s.

Corfe Castle, Swanage Railway: BR Class 4MT 2-6-4T 80104 departs Corfe Castle with a late morning train for Swanage, passing Class 08 08436, 10 September 2006.

Castles necessarily dominated their territory in order to provide the best view for defence against any marauding enemy and Corfe clearly fulfilled this role, as its partly intact ruins demonstrate. Not that there would be any need for concern to its watchful garrison from the busy trains arriving and departing below it, which in fact help to alleviate the steady flow of road traffic carrying the hordes of tourists passing through the nearby village on their way to and from 'invading' the seaside at Swanage. The Class 08 unwittingly enhances this recreation of a scene from the 1960s, and the exhaust from the chimney of 80104 on this warm day fortunately doesn't obliterate the view of the fortress.

Corfe Common, Swanage Railway: leading locomotive LSWR Class M7 0-4-4T 30053 and rear locomotive GWR 0-6-2T 5600 Class 6695 in push/pull mode with the 13.04 Harman's Cross to Norden, 12 September 2010.

The early autumn browns of the dry bracken and the tapestry created by the intermittent blue sky and clouds that mingle with the authentic Southern green carriages and varied locomotive liveries here provide a reminiscent scene of push/pull operations in the past. Of course, use of autocoaches and steam rail motors precluded such a need for provision of a locomotive at each end on branch lines where run-around facilities were not easily located at relevant termini. Modernisation saw diesel multiple units as the answer and clearly, with a need for two locomotive crews, the sort of train formation shown was certainly expensive and likely unprofitable. However, the passengers conveyed here would fully approve of such exuberance! Both locomotives appear to be working quite hard, although they will soon be able to ease in their efforts as Corfe Castle station looms into view.

Near Harman's Cross, Swanage Railway: GWR 4-6-0 7800 Class 'Manor' 7802 *Bradley Manor* hauls the 14.30... Swanage to Norden. Preserved at the Severn Valley Railway, 12 September 2010.

Whether the appearance of a Great Western steam locomotive on a route which was strictly LSWR has any relevance to the group of walkers in the field to the rear of the scene remains a mystery. Certainly they would surely have been impressed by the sturdy appearance of this magnificently restored steam locomotive as it steadily climbs towards Corfe. In steam days, 'Manor' Class locomotives were not a feature on such branch lines as this in the South Dorset landscape and yet, at a stretch of imagination, we could be in Cambrian territory where these locomotives would have been quite at home. Indeed *Bradley Manor* was based in its earlier life at Bristol from where it was used on cross country work around Wiltshire, Dorset, Somerset and South Wales. Certainly this locomotive exudes all the character and ambience that made it the pride of the GWR, and it rightly deserves the accolades of the myriad photographers lucky enough to capture this superb machine in action during its years in preservation.

Near Harman's Cross, Swanage Railway: leading locomotive GWR 0-6-2T 5600 Class 6695 and train locomotive LBSCR 0-6-0T Class A1X Terrier 32662 *Martello*, are seen paired together for ... the 15.30... Norden to Harman's Cross, 12 September 2010.

Crossing an almost bleak landscape with one solitary tree standing sentry to the rear of the train as it passes some typical lineside huts, we could be forgiven for suggesting this to be a remote outpost of some distant rural railway branch line. It is merely some open chalkland astride an area of rolling arable and livestock farmland that characterises this part of the Isle of Purbeck – and we are not far from the sparkle of the Atlantic lapping at the coastline of such geological marvels as Lulworth Cove, Durdle Door and Chesil Beach.

The train consist is intriguing, for *Martello* is rarely seen away from its preservation home at the Bressingham Steam Museum. Earlier in the afternoon it had run out of steam at Harman's Cross and therefore was being kept within the shuttle formation that runs at gala events between Norden and Harman's Cross. Paired with 6695 it is assured a part in the remaining afternoon's timetabled trains, and provides a splendid companion for comparison. The Southern green coaches form an appropriate consist, even though they highlight the diminutive tank locomotive's smaller dimensions. In view of the fact that this design of locomotive was intended for light railways such as those found on the Isle of Wight, we could almost say that this scene could have been one found on that charming island's railways, if we can excuse the Great Western locomotive's co-appearance! Could it be that those wisps of cloud in the background are really steam exhaust from *Martello*?

Toddington, Gloucestershire Warwickshire Steam Railway: Port Talbot Railway GWR 0-6-0ST 813 in shunting movement with a gunpowder van and 'Toad' brake van, 2 June 2007.

Here we see a reminder of the time when specialist wagons for high-risk goods formed part of the railway scene. It is interesting to note that a requirement for display on gunpowder vans was a rectangular metal plate mounted on the door bearing a set of standard instructions regarding the use of 'nailless overboots' (to avoid sparks) and deterring the running of the van through a goods shed. Shunting gunpowder vans into goods sheds was generally prohibited, and understandably when any loading or unloading took place on railway property, such would have been carried out well away from everything else in the yard. In peacetime a maximum of five gunpowder vans could be included in a single train. In wartime entire trains might be made up of gunpowder vans with some open wagons also pressed into service. I suppose our modern-day equivalent might be the safe handling of the nuclear flask trains that operate to and from Sellafield nuclear reprocessing plant.

Near Toddington, Gloucestershire Warwickshire Railway: GWR 4500 Class 2-6-2T 5542 with autocoach 178 provides the 17.00 from Toddington to Winchcombe, 2 June 2007.

Here is a reminder that economies of scale were very much in the minds of the railway companies when it came to rural branch line services. Incorporating a driving cab at the end of an attached coach while using a modified tank locomotive meant there was no need to spend time shunting around a set of carriages at station termini when the requirements of the anticipated number of passengers could be met in this alternative way. The driver operated the locomotive controls from the autocoach cab using a series of linkages underneath the autocoach frame. In order to control the engine, he could apply the brakes and also manipulate the regulator on the locomotive. Some railway companies preferred a single self-contained powered passenger coach, usually referred to as a 'railmotor'. The GWR preferred a standard single driving coach design for these duties, and up to two could be coupled together, or one placed either side of the locomotive, which worked in push-pull mode.

Several of these autocoaches are preserved in working order. The chocolate and cream of the Great Western autocoach certainly complements the Great Western green of the locomotive. Passengers can choose to sit either longitudinally or in conventional facing seats, and can therefore choose the type of view they prefer.

Near Gretton, Gloucestershire Warwickshire Steam Railway: Southern Railway 4-6-2 'West Country Pacific' 34007 *Wadebridge* departs Greet tunnel with the 15.30 Toddington to Cheltenham, 2 June 2007.

Emerging triumphant into the spring daylight, the bankside flowers greet this welcome guest to the Gloucestershire Warwickshire Steam Railway. Judging by the heads leaning out from the windows it is proving very popular. The disc head codes indicate it is recreating an express passenger train – although the end of the line at the racecourse will terminate such intentions to reach south of Cheltenham. Perhaps the locomotive is the racehorse galloping towards the finish after encountering all the hurdles en route such as the dark and dingy tunnel from which it has escaped in evident full flight.

Above: Llangollen, Llangollen Railway: GWR 'City' 3700 Class 4-4-0 3440 *City of Truro* with empty coaching stock shunting movement, 18 April 2009.

We glimpse into the cab of this immaculate locomotive which continues to impress each generation of steam railway enthusiasts and technical engineers alike. There is a grace to its movement and the sleek lines of the frame and boiler combine to make a superb shape in which to contain the details of the design. There's just the right amount of steam emitted to create an atmosphere of business, and a full tender of coal promises there will be plenty of effort and determination to haul the coaches filled with their collection of admirers including those who seek to enjoy the thrill of capturing such an accomplished locomotive at work. After all, this was the first locomotive to have been 'officially' recorded as reaching a speed of over 100mph while hauling a five-vehicle 'Ocean Mail' special from Plymouth to Paddington. It may indeed be a disputed claim but who is to dispute *City of Truro*'s magnificence and glamour as a representative of a vintage class of steam locomotive. The fact that it was posed alongside Truro Cathedral in the summer of 2004 suggests it deserves and receives the same respect as that we give to our other most valued items of heritage architecture. This photograph of the locomotive was taken when it featured at the very special 'Steel, Steam and Stars' event in 2009.

Opposite: Deeside Halt, Llangollen Railway: GWR 5101 Class 2-6-2T 5199 departs with the 10.42 Carrog to Llangollen freight, 18 April 2009.

This rural springtime scene and train formation could be a timeless reflection on steam days found in parts of Devon – though the height of the hills asserts the more accurate location as Denbighshire in Wales. The unfitted freight clunks and clatters as it is hauled up the gradient by its labouring 'Large Prairie' Class of locomotive – a type most commonly seen on suburban and local passenger traffic. There is very little in the photograph to place it in the modern day and it recalls the times when local freight went by rail for merging with longer mixed freight trains for conveyance to intended markets or merchants rather than being carried in lengthy lorries which can't easily be overtaken on valley roads or mountain passes. It was all labour intensive and here the fireman will be working hard while the driver keeps an eye on the rails ahead. Theirs was (and still is) a job well done and in which they took pride. Our modern fast-paced world could benefit from an occasional pause for thought and reflection on such a level of commitment.

River Dee Valley, Llangollen Railway: Stanier design LMS Class 5MT 4-6-0 44806 (running as 44801) runs alongside the River Dee with the 14.00 Llangollen to Carrog, 18 April 2009.

In some ways this scene recalls a suburban locomotive hauling a workers' train of slam-door commuter stock that might best suit an industrial landscape, such as that found in the towns and cities of the north-west, rather than here in these sylvan surroundings. The train pulls away from the curve alongside the river with aplomb as it heads onwards into the fine countryside of the Dee Valley's rolling hills. Spring foliage and blossom has arrived and the lambing season is underway. There is an almost carefree atmosphere that welcomes the warmth of the springtime sun and the railway has the valley to itself, away from the busy road higher up the hillside.

Between Glyndyfrdwy and Carrog, Llangollen Railway: GWR 0-6-0PT 6400 Class 6430 in push-pull mode with autotrailer coaches heading for Carrog, 18 April 2009.

This authentic auto-sandwich features another method of push-pull formation that appealed to the GWR's rural branch operations as referred to in a previous photograph of this type of train. The attraction for those travelling on board was that you could choose to sit behind the driver at the very front and see the view of the line ahead , or view the line from the rear auto as it receded away into the distance. If seated longitudinally, you had a panorama through the side-on windows. Later on, diesel multiple units provided this kind of experience – but without the hiss and push of the pistons as the steam locomotive trundled its merry way through the countryside. Its lilting sound and rocking motion might well assist in a quick doze for the weary traveller who has connected into the train for an onward connection home, or to maybe to visit a relative. Mind you, just look at that glorious scenery they'd be missing …

River Dee Valley, Llangollen Railway: LNER D49/1 Class 246 *Morayshire* runs alongside the River Dee with an afternoon freight from Carrog to Llangollen, 18 April 2009.

Now here is a truly rare visitor that was a guest of the very special Llangollen Railway 'Steel, Steam and Stars 2' event that drew locomotives from preserved railways across the UK. A taste of Scotland's distinctive steed of steam locomotives, *Morayshire* was completed at Darlington in February 1928 and from 1928 to nationalisation was shedded at Dundee, Perth, Haymarket and Edinburgh St Margaret's locomotive bases. The class was designed for intermediate express passenger duties in the north-east and Scotland, while owing to a need for economy a 4-4-0 wheel arrangement was chosen over a possibly more logical 4-4-2 ('Atlantic') wheel arrangement. The LNER apple green livery shines spectacularly and the interesting, if intriguing, wheel arrangement is clear to see. At this location, we could indeed be in Aberdeenshire or parts of Perthshire unless we hear the distinctive Welsh tongue of the locals deployed. Quite what they would think of such a Scottish interloper amidst their landscape we don't need to be concerned about, for admiration and applause are surely and inevitably their response.

Between Glyndyfrdwy and Carrog, Llangollen Railway: LMS Class 5MT 4-6-0 44806 hauls the 16.12 Carrog to Llangollen, 18 April 2009.

The interesting coach next to the locomotive is Beavertail observation car 1719E, one of two observation cars built at Doncaster in 1937 for the 'Coronation' high speed train services between London and Edinburgh. It would have been accustomed to haulage by A4 locomotives. Eventually it found use helping travellers on the West Highland lines to enjoy the best of Scottish scenery. It looks resplendent as restored in the maroon livery which was applied after it was rebuilt by BR at Cowlairs works in 1959. Its continued existence is all thanks to Railway Vehicle Preservations, the historic carriage restoration group based on the Great Central Railway. It is hoped that the occupants of the carriage are more impressed than are the grazing sheep.

Shackerstone, Battlefield Railway: 0-4-0ST 2648 *Linda*, built 1940 by Bagnall, in a light engine movement, Sunday 28 October 2007.

This station oozes Midland red: bricks, platforms, luggage cases, trolley handles, seats, metal panels, window frames. The viewer may wish to add further. The black iron columns and decor complement the black locomotive with its red outline further echoing the Midland theme. This interesting locomotive was built by Bagnall, a Staffordshire company; it was the first of a batch of nine supplied to the Ministry of Supply for use at Royal Ordnance factories, and later at the Dunlop Rubber Company's Erdington Works. Until 1957 it had been oil-fired but was later fitted with a coal-fired boiler. The miniature lanterns strung along above the guttering are pertinent to forthcoming Halloween.

Near Foley Park, Severn Valley Railway: West Country Class 34027 *Taw Valley* running as 34036 *Westward Ho* with an afternoon train from Bridgnorth to Kidderminster, 15 October 2005.

Highlighted by the golden hues of the bracken, *Taw Valley* strolls up the gradient towards Foley Park tunnel offering a significant distraction to any of the diners enjoying their food in the adjacent restaurant car. Clearly at least a couple of enthusiasts next to open windows are enjoying the sounds emitted by this magnificent beast. One can only conjecture how Bulleid, as chief mechanical engineer of the Southern Railway and designer of this Pacific, might have regarded such a Great Western carriage featuring in the multitudinous formations that composed the 'Atlantic Coast Express' – with which this locomotive would have been familiar. Perhaps he would, as must we, allow for such incompatibility in view of the fact that it is here proudly enjoying the rolling contours and heritage of one of the top pedigree of preserved railways; one on which his locomotive can really stretch its legs.

Opposite: Falling Sands Viaduct, Severn Valley Railway: Class 4MT 80079 hauls a set of Gresley teak coaches across the Staffordshire and Worcestershire Canal, Bridgnorth, 28 December 2000.

A seasonally cool spell of weather has frozen the canal – a reminder of one of the reasons why railways replaced canals for transporting goods and merchandise. Frozen points at railway junctions can be provided with heaters and the snow poses no problem to the train apart from some slippery rails, though station platform surfaces will be inevitably slippery. The welcome rays of the winter's sun are not strong enough to melt the snow which will remain for several days. We may be close to a busy town bustling with Christmas sales shoppers but the serenity of this location allows this photographer a calm retreat and a rewarding reminiscence of railways in years past.

Below: Bridgnorth, Severn Valley Railway: Class 9F 2-10-0 92212 arrives mid-afternoon amidst a winter countryside scene, 28 December 2000.

The River Severn slowly flows through a snow-clad landscape in which the shivering trees huddle together for shelter from the forthcoming icy night. The snow on the carriage roofs has remained throughout the journey from Kidderminster, although no doubt the passengers are warmed by the seasonal refreshments offered on board. The glint of the afternoon sun has virtually no impact on the cold metal of the locomotive, though the crew will enjoy the frequent blasts of warm air permitted into the cab whenever coal is fed into the firebox. It's all a reminder of how main line steam battled through the very cold winter of 1963 when, for sixty-two consecutive days, snow lay on the ground in the South of England. Climate change means similar events are very rare, and opportunities to recreate the experience of a preserved steam train enduring winter conditions far fewer.

Damems, Keighley and Worth Valley Railway: BR Standard Class 4MT 2-6-4T 80002 passes en route to Haworth and Oxenhope, June 2006.

A scene reflecting the character of its location within Brontë Country as a non-stop service passes the platform-based signal box and waiting room, all in appropriately authentic LMS livery. It helps recapture the branch line semi-fast services that were sometimes provided for rush hour commuters who were not requiring trains which stopped at every halt and consequently took absolutely ages to complete their journey up the line. Most prevalent in the Home Counties, these tended to help fit into timetables such extra services along mainly single-line routes linking the countryside villages with the various opportunities offered in the nearby towns. Such practice is still evident elsewhere on such lines as the Exeter to Barnstaple route. The overall line speed would dictate how fast such semi-fast services could complete their journey. Occasionally, some preserved lines will operate non-stop services, often those such as dining trains which have no need to set down or pick up casual passengers, with the time on board taken up by waiter service of various mouthwatering courses provided on the menu while diners enjoy their meal at a relaxing pace.

Plym Valley Railway: cycle path near Cann Wood Viaduct in winter light, 21 January 2020.

A tribute to many long-closed railways where once steam prevailed is their increasing use as cycleways and footpaths linking towns and villages via a different mode of motive power! It's variable as to how much previous railway infrastructure remains in place, with some routes having scarce evidence of their links with rail history while others may have fully restored stations now used as private residences. Along the Plym Valley section of cycle path from Marsh Mills to Yelverton, part of the ex-GWR branch, now branded 'Drake's Trail', there are no less than four impressive viaducts, one tunnel, several overbridges, cuttings and various disused platforms. It also passes alongside two reinstated stations at either end of a section of preserved line belonging to the Plym Valley Railway. During one winter's visit cycling along this route, the author encountered icicles measuring three metres, hanging from inside the aforementioned tunnel, where water from the ground constantly leaks through the roof. They were melting and falling somewhat precipitously to the ground thus creating a skating rink. The path climbs steadily towards the edge of Dartmoor and provides a reminder to cyclists and walkers of the feats of engineering required to facilitate the progress of those steam locomotives which consistently honoured their occasional description as 'the iron horse'.

Chapter 5
FINALE

Crowcombe Heathfield Station: West Somerset Railway, 29 December 2005.

The last trains will soon arrive and depart from the snow-clad platforms which will then fall silent as the cold winter's night brings its mist and freezing chill. The rails glint gently in the twilight and reflect a warming glow from the semaphores and platform lights, while the tungsten yellow lighting in the signal box adds further aura. It's a calm and timeless scene. There's even a couple of large Christmas star decorations above the right-hand seat. Our journey has reached its end and we can use the forthcoming winter's evenings to dream of or reflect on our own visits within Britain's varied blend of attractive landscapes. Whither shall we travel to find the gems and treasures that await us? For all of life is a journey – it's for us to venture in search of that next goal, a spiritual quest awaiting the fulfilment that only we can realise. How fortunate that we are to be able to contemplate such scenic splendours as we venture out as pilgrims towards that future golden treasure.

BIBLIOGRAPHY

Backtrack, Vol. 4, No. 6, Atlantic Transport Publishers.

BR Gradient Main Line Profiles, Ian Allan Publishing, 2003.

Curtis, A.N., *Western Liveries*, A & C Services, 2001.

Heritage Railway, Issue 134, Mortons Media Group Limited, 2010.

Jones, Mervyn, *The Essential Guide to Welsh Heritage and Scenic Railways*, The Oakwood Press, 2010.

Kay, Peter, *Rails Along the Sea Wall*, Platform 5 Publishing Ltd, 1990.

Marshall, J., *The Guinness Book of Rail Facts and Feats*, Guinness Superlatives Limited, 1979.

Pritchard, R. and Hall, P., *Preserved Locomotives of British Railways*, 18th edn, Platform 5 Publishing Ltd, 2018.

Rail Express, Issues 162 (November 2009), 165 (February 2010), 167 (April 2010), 168 (May 2010), Mortons Media Group Limited.

Railways Illustrated, September 2009, Ian Allan Publishing.